What the Experts Are Saying About *Punctuation Plain and Simple*

"Very successful and practical contribution...maintains a nice balance between rules that most of us still obey, on the one hand, and those many variations on the rules that are responses to oral speech, on the other hand. An up-to-date treatment of a tricky subject, and it should be a useful guide to writers in many fields of endeavor."

—Walker Gibson, former president of the National Council of Teachers of English (NCTE)

"This book reveals why the author is a master of the craft of using punctuation as an aid to writing clearly. The text serves as a trustworthy source for the novice, as well as the professional writer, who wants to communicate precisely and accurately. I am pleased to find that Professor Alward deals not only with the orthodox and standard uses of punctuation but also includes illustrations of contemporary uses of this system of writing signs that help us to communicate unambiguously. When I do any writing, I always have *Punctuation Plain and Simple* within reach, along with a thesaurus, a dictionary, and an American-English usage guide."

—Wallace L. Goldstein, Ph.D., author of *Teaching English as a Second Language* and "The Fringe Benefits of Writing"

"Any professional putting pen to paper or finger to keyboard can avoid either embarrassment or wasting time simply by keeping *Punctuation Plain and Simple* in easy reach. It's a rule book that reads less like a rule book than a conversation with the authors. I love it."

—Jim Trelease, author of *The Read-Aloud Handbook*

Punctuation Plain and Simple

By
Edgar C. Alward
and
Jean A. Alward

CAREER PRESS

Franklin Lakes, NJ

PUNCTUATION PLAIN AND SIMPLE
Cover design by The Hub Graphics Corp.
Printed in the U.S.A. by Book-mart Press

To order this title, please call toll-free 1-800-CAREER-1 (NJ and Canada: 201-848-0310) to order using VISA or Master Card, or for further information on books from Career Press.

The Career Press, Inc., 3 Tice Road, PO Box 687, Franklin Lakes, NJ 07417

Library of Congress Cataloging-in-Publication Data

Alward, Edgar C., 1921-
    Punctuation plain and simple / by Edgar C. Alward and Jean A. Alward.
        p.   cm.
    Includes index.
    ISBN 1-56414-274-4 (pbk.)
    1. English language--Punctuation.   I. Alward, Jean A., 1936-
II. Title.
PE1450.A54   1997
421'.1--dc21   96-51152
                                                                          CIP

Acknowledgments

Many of my students and colleagues at Westfield (Massachusetts) State College have made suggestions and special contributions to this book on punctuation. Much of the book is an almost nongrammatical approach based on the original editions titled *Punctuation: A Rationale of American Practice,* copyrighted in 1966 and again in 1967. I am still indebted to Dr. Meg Colo, then my student assistant at the college, for the index that I continued to use in the 1988 edition, authored by me and my youngest son Dale, as well as in this edition.

Dale contributed a younger-student view of the book as we co-authored the much-needed simplified, almost nongrammatical approach. Among the many examples are the autobiographical ones and the Miss Piggy ones by one of my former students, JulieAnn Wolowicz.

Many others have helped to make this book what it is today. Over a period of 30 years, colleagues, students, friends, and family have in some way contributed to its content. The combination of suggestions, comments, and questions posed by Betsy Sheldon and Suzanne Gruber at Career Press was the catalyst that helped Jean and me to finalize this book. *Punctuation Plain and Simple* will now be even more helpful to all writers not only in improving their punctuation skills but also in refining the structure and creativity of their verbal messages.

My co-author, my wife Jean, is also an authority in the field of punctuation and grammar. Whereas I may overlook an error or lack of clarity in my pedagogical presentation, she is able to produce correctness and better syntax for the student's comprehension.

—Edgar C. Alward, 1997

Contents

Preface

Those of us who teach English have tried to teach students to punctuate correctly—a difficult objective in a changing medium where rules tend to be only temporary. Most English teachers are concerned with students' problems in writing—problems that students have not only in syntax but also in punctuation. To some degree the problems with punctuation may be caused by the lack of a system used by so many writers, printers, and publishers. Our lack of success in helping students may be mainly due to their ignorance of the grammatical terms used to explain the structure of the sentence. Traditionally, a teacher practically beat the terms and concepts into a student's head by means of repetition and memorization. Perhaps another way to remedy this ignorance, as well as make up for technical or creative fluctuations, is to provide an alternative method of determining punctuation for those students unfamiliar with the language structure.

Our purpose in this book is to provide a method of understanding punctuation based on an analysis of how today's writers and publishers punctuate. This understanding is coupled with a learn-by-doing approach. Our analyses of advertisements taken from the three media—television, radio, and print—have provided us with considerable insight. Punctuation marks for the written word convey at least a similar meaning to that conveyed by the intonation patterns of the spoken word. The objective of a new punctuation book, therefore, is to establish guidelines so that written punctuation gains more efficiency in conveying an intended meaning to the reader, just as one would convey meaning to the listener by intonation in the spoken language.

Speaking for one of us, I, Edgar, have been studying the uses of punctuation for more than 40 years. In the last 30 years I became very intent in analyzing sentence structures in publications by reputable publishers to determine a rationale. Within this time I published two editions of a book titled *Punctuation: A Rationale of American Practice.* Because so few have written about punctuation, I have had to depend mostly upon primary or original research. I have continued to exhaust all indexes by studying the traditional graphic system of the marks of punctuation, as well as the punctuation used by contemporary publishers.

All writers know that common feeling of a work never reaching its completion. Those of us involved in this project share this impression; many questions are still open regarding what we have included. Because we emphasize the importance of cultural changes within punctuation and have resolved ourselves to take these into account in our work, we welcome any comments you have to provide. Please direct all comments to:

Edgar and Jean Alward
69 Pine Island Lake
Westhampton, MA 01027
Phone: 413-527-5172
Fax: 413-527-6032
e-mail: edgar.a lward@the-spa.com

Introduction

In the early English comedy *Ralph Roister Doister,* Ralph asks a scribe to prepare a love letter for Dame Custance, an attractive widow whom he is courting. Ralph intends for the letter to read:

Sweete mistresse, where as I love you,
nothing at all
Regarding your substance and richesse;
chief of all
For your personage, beautie, demeanour
and wit
I commend me unto you, never a whit
Soria to hear report of your good welfare.

The letter is prepared by the scribe and is eventually read to the lady by Ralph's friend Merrygreeke. To the lady's shock and amazement, the tone of the letter of devotion is far from endearing:

Sweete mistresse, where as I love you
nothing at all;
Regarding your substance and richesse
chief of all,
For your personage, beautie, demeanour and
wit,

> I commend me unto you never a whit.
> Soria to hear report of your good welfare.

Ralph becomes highly indignant that he has been so badly let down because of Merrygreeke's reading of the letter. Consequently, he takes the letter back to the scribe, who declares:

> Then was it as ye prayed to have it, I wot
> But in reading and pointing, there was
> made some fault.

Misuse of punctuation can cause costly errors as illustrated in a tariff bill passed by the Forty-second United States Congress in 1872. The bill intended to exempt certain items from duty, among which were "fruit-plants, tropical and semitropical for the purpose of propagation and cultivation." The clerk who transcribed the bill mistakenly converted the hyphen to a comma, thus causing the bill to read "fruit, plants, tropical and semi-tropical..." This meant that some fruits *and* all plants in the tropical and semi-tropical categories could be allowed into the country free of duty. The error was not corrected until the following session of Congress in 1874 and, consequently, cost the United States Government an estimated $2 million in lawsuits and in duties not received.

For writing to be clear to the reader, it must be punctuated according to the standards recognized by the society for which it is intended. In England a comma has usually been placed between the number and the street, making it, for example, 10, *Downing Street;* while in the United States, we would write 10 *Downing Street.* When the Americans write *6/10/97,* they mean *June 10, 1997;* however, when the English write *6/10/97,* they mean "the sixth day of October 1997." In the United States today, the *6/10/97* is giving way to the more specific *10 June 1997.*

The English hyphenate *to-day*, *to-night*, and *to-morrow*, a practice that has long disappeared in the United States.

The English tend to be more particular about apostrophes in the possessive forms of nouns, while Americans seem to hope that by ignoring them they will go away. It is apparent, though, that the use of the apostrophe will eventually disappear. A cautious rule may be "When in doubt, leave it out!" But let's be careful not to ignore the specific rules explained in this book or we may be as badly misunderstood as Merrygreeke caused Ralph to be.

Both punctuation and sentence-pattern arrangement contribute substantially to the meaning of a piece of prose. The order in which information is laid down into sentences determines the exactness of the meaning. As punctuation provides a cadence of pauses and stops, the reader's comprehension is enhanced—moreover clarified. Cadence is defined in *The Random House College Dictionary* in several ways, two of which are:

> 1. Rhythmic flow of a sequence of sounds or words;...4. The flow or rhythm of events, especially the pattern in which something is experienced.

Without punctuation marks, reading would be a very difficult task, as it must have been for the earliest readers. Most of the earliest written records appear to have had no spacing between words, no capitals, no indentation, and no punctuation marks. Writing went something like this:

> mostoftheearliestwrittenrecordsappearto
> havehadnospacingbetweenwordsnocapitals
> noindentationsandnopunctuationmarks

It has been said that if man had no marks of punctuation, he would eventually invent some. This has evidently been true ever since man attempted to set his ideas down in some form of writing. There is some evidence that the caveman in his carvings on the walls attempted a form of punctuation, as he separated his characters or words from each other by a period or dot.

Although early humans made some attempt to separate their words, the early Greeks, as advanced as they were, had no punctuation marks, no capitals, and no spacing between words. By the fourth century, however, they were using dots and other arbitrary symbols to set off individual words. The use of these symbols by the Greeks gave our modern civilization some of its ideas about punctuation, for the names of our punctuation marks came from the Greeks. The word *period* comes from the Greek word *periodos* (circuit, period of time, rhetorical period), which in turn was derived from the two words *peri* (round, about) and *hodos* (way), indicating a cycle. The word *comma* is derived from the Greek word *komma* (segment, clause) which came from the word *koptein* (to cut), meaning "a piece to be cut," such as phrases and clauses. The word *colon* comes from the Greek word *kolon* (a limb), such as the transition point of the sentence. Later, printers used the punctuation marks of the Greek grammarians but with some alterations; for example, the Greek interrogation mark (;) became our modern semicolon.

Aristophanes of Byzantium (257?-180? BC), a Greek grammarian, critic, and librarian at Alexandria in Egypt, is credited with having developed the regular system of punctuation used by the Greeks. It was he who used dots or small circles at various levels (high, middle, low) to indicate the pauses later associated with the period, the comma, and the semicolon.

In the centuries following the Greek invention of punctuation, there appears to have been no orderly system used. Punctuation marks were seldom used by writers or copyists in classical Latin because of the significant pauses represented by special constructions, such as the enclitic *que*, which served as a comma. By the year AD 650, words were regularly separated from each other in manuscript. In the time of Alcuin (735-804), the leader of Charlemagne's Palace School, still further regularity was attained. Yet during the Middle Ages little of this regularity was practiced; and by the 13th century, uniformity in the use of punctuation was virtually nonexistent.

Little was done about punctuation again until the 16th century. Even William Caxton (1424?-1491), known to be the first British printer, had no particular system of punctuation. He used a system of slanting lines to indicate pauses between sentences and sentence elements. The following quotation from Caxton's edition of Sir Thomas Malory's (?-1471) *Morte D'Arthur* illustrates the spelling and capitalization of that time and another mark of punctuation—the paragraph sign.

¶Thus endeth thys noble and Joyous Book
entytled Le Morte D'Arthur / Notwythſtanding
    it treateth of the byrth / lyſ / and actes
    of the ſaid Kyng Arthur of his noble
knyghtes of the rounde table / theyr marvayllous
enquestes and adventures / thachyavyng of the
ſangreal /....

Aldus Manutius (1449-1515), an Italian printer who published small-sized books in order to make them available at a lower cost, probably did more than anyone up to that time to systematize punctuation; and many printers adopted his improvisations.

Although Manutius did much toward systematizing punctuation, it did not become standardized as we know it today—in the United States, at least—until the middle of the 19th century. For the 20th-century reader, works originally printed prior to 1850 are now usually modernized in their punctuation and spelling. For example, copies of the Declaration of Independence appear with the modern *s* instead of the *f*; the modern version also does not have the period plus dash (.—) and the colon plus dash (:—) that were written into the original document.

Another example of punctuation that would be considered irregular today is the close punctuation used in the 17th and 18th centuries. Sentences were elaborately speckled with commas, colons, semicolons, and parentheses. For example, commas were used to separate subject from predicate, modifier from the word modified, restrictive as well as nonrestrictive clauses from the main clause—a style that was perfectly acceptable to writers of that period.

Grammarians of the 18th century thought of the comma as a pause for a count of one; the semicolon, for a count of two; the colon, for a count of three; and the period, for a count of four—a theory based upon oratorical pauses. John Wilson wrote that this elocutionary theory seemed to consider punctuation "as being the representatives only of rhetorical pauses...." Even today many writers and English teachers punctuate strictly according to sound.

When Richard Hoe (1826-1886) invented the rotary press around the middle of the 19th century, reading material became available to a greater number of people. Consequently, as reading became more prevalent, grammarians such as Wilson in his *Treatise on English Punctuation* (1850) began to recognize the need for a grammatical method of punctuation applicable to silent reading:

> ...on the whole, it will be found that the art
> of Punctuation is founded rather on
> grammar than on rhetoric; that its chief aim
> is to unfold the meaning of sentences, with

> the least trouble to the reader; and that it
> aids the delivery, only in so far as it tends to
> bring out the sense of the writer to the best
> advantage.

Contemporary punctuation usage is a matter of custom, changing less rapidly than dress or manners obviously, but nonetheless changing over the decades. We like to think the uses are based upon some practical, as well as rational, standard. With this in mind, the most valuable use of this manual is to learn the rules of punctuation in order that you may utilize the marks of punctuation as governed by *our* present "logical" standard.

Yet, all traditional uses considered, "rules are made to be broken," to use an old saying. Once the techniques of writing and punctuation are learned and mastered, they become tools with which creativity may take place—a creativity that might require stretching those rules in order to achieve a specific effect. Beware, though, that breaking the rules is not an end in itself. Any variation from the standard puts a responsibility on your shoulders to make sure your reader comprehends and appreciates your creative variation. To attain this creativity, you must first learn to apply intelligently the tools of the writer.

Because every form of writing benefits from logic and clarity, we hope that this study of punctuation marks and their uses provides a good set of "tools" for whatever you choose to write. The book is designed to give you "hands-on" experience in punctuating prose. For this purpose, exercises are woven into each section. We hope that you experience some fun in your writing, but at the same time, take the rules seriously enough to learn more about the specific marks they illustrate.

1

Terminal marks

Today, as sentences tend to become shorter and as writers tend to use the open style of punctuation that requires as few marks as possible, the period is beginning to catch up in frequency with the most widely used punctuation mark, the comma. Obviously, most sentences end with a period. Occasionally, a sentence may end with either a question mark or an exclamation mark. In this section, we will look at sentences and the marks used to finish them off, and then we will assess some sentences that don't quite fit the traditional forms with which we have become familiar.

Before we discuss terminal *marks*, we would like to mention a typing habit that often distracts readers: double spacing at the end of sentences. Many of those who teach typing are still teaching this obsolete practice. However, with the advent of the computer and the word processor came changes that affect all who ever learned to type on a typewriter. "What is the difference?" you may ask. Read a business letter done on a typewriter and one done on a computer by someone who double spaces at the end of each sentence. The letter done on the computer—with justified margins—has wide gaps between the words and sentences. Fortunately, some of the newer computers are addressing this old typing habit. One typist recently protested that her new computer forced her to allow only one space at the end of the sentences that she was typing. Having said that, let's move on to our discussion of terminal marks.

The declarative sentence

The traditional declarative sentence is a simple assertion that expresses a complete thought. This is the most basic of sentences as it is purely informational in form. The declarative sentence ends with a period.

> The dorm girls do their assignments in the lounge.

The interrogative sentence

Like the declarative sentence, the interrogative sentence expresses a complete thought, but it warns the readers that you have asked them something as it probes for more information. It ends with a question mark.

> Why do the dorm girls do their assignments in the lounge?

The exclamatory sentence

The exclamatory sentence is one that asserts a forcefulness like a shout or an emphatic tone of voice. Similar to the declarative sentence, a thought may also be completely expressed with an exclamatory sentence. The exclamation mark is used for this type of sentence.

What a place to do their assignments!

It is a good idea to be sparing in your use of the exclamation mark as it can easily be overused. Exclamation marks sprinkled freely throughout a composition can be similar in effect to a speech permeated with shouts and emphatic gestures. The speaker or writer is rendered as giddy and overexcited. This overuse of the exclamation point can tarnish the integrity of the writing.

The imperative sentence

The fourth of the traditional sentences, the imperative sentence, resembles the declarative sentence in that it generally ends with a period, but unlike the declarative sentence, it usually expresses a command or a simple request.

Do your assignments in the lounge.

Obviously, in the imperative sentence, the subject "you" or "will you" is understood. This omission of the subject is the exception or condition that keeps the imperative sentence alive.

The verbless sentence

Groups of words that may appear incomplete are often expressed as complete thoughts by the writer. More traditionally, these are known as interjections (or exclamatory remarks) and elliptical expressions. These constructions can be terminated in a variety of ways.

> Horrors! In the lounge. Why in the lounge?
> Usually one roommate or the other decides to
> entertain in the dorm room!

Until the 1970s, the verbless structures were more likely to appear in narrative than in expository writing.

However, contemporary writers of advertisements and technical material have become more informal in their use of fragments. If the author has an "ear" for conversational writing, the application of fragments can be very effective. In the following paragraph, only the topic sentence is a complete statement—the others are fragments.

> The best thing about college is a boy. A boy with whom you can talk over all your little problems concerning grades, homework, etc. A boy who you know will listen attentively and who will calmly give you advice because he is older and wiser. A boy whom you can trust not to disclose any of the little secrets you and he share. A boy with whom you can walk through the campus at any time of the year just taking in the beauty of nature and loving every minute of the walk, simply because you are with him. A boy whom you can look up to because he is all you consider to be good and right. A boy with whom you can be proud to go to school functions, because you know he will always make a good impression on anyone you may meet. A boy from whom you can take any "ranks" about your size or any of your other faults. But mainly a boy in whom you place ever a hope, every dream, and all your faith.
>
> —Joyce Gunn

If the author of the preceding paragraph had corrected her fragments, she probably would have lost some of the effect of her innovations.

In a very different sense to the foregoing narrative, yet equally effective, is the use of fragments in the following advertisements.

Every part of your body has its daily requirement. Now, for the first time, you're about to experience a new shampoo—HDR—specifically formulated.

Anything can affect this requirement. Like too much humidity. Or over-conditioning. This extra-body formula is so scientifically advanced, it can change its action as it cleanses—rebalancing your hair's body, shine, and manageability. Adding extra-luxurious fullness to even limp, fine hair. Working to make your hair the best it can be. Day by day.

⇒ *Of course, much of this advertisement's effect is in its appearance on a bottle of HDR shampoo, rather than abstractly in some other form of literature.*

Another example:

Room 564. Want to see what they have in common besides the same address?

Arbitrary variations of sentence endings

It is important to note, however, that the terminal marks usually applied to the four traditional sentences may vary somewhat. In a sentence that appears declarative, the writer may intend to have an interrogative meaning.

All sentences must be complete statements? Nonsense!

A rhetorical question, which may be simply a polite request, ends with a period.

> Will you please forward our mail to the new address.

⇒ *The words "will you" simply softens the command "please forward."*

A sentence may be declarative, interrogative, or imperative in form and yet be felt by the writer to be exclamatory.

> The barn next to the burning house will burst into flames!

> Could you be on time!

> Do every lesson that is assigned!

The imperative sentence tends to have a slightly different meaning than its counterpart, the declarative sentence, which can only be determined by the tone in which it is expressed. In the following examples, the first two sentences contain imperative statements. The last three sentences appear to be a form of the interrogative. However, the slight variation in syntactical structure, along with different end marks, produces in each one a different tone. Becoming aware of the tonal aspect of writing introduces the novice to the most difficult part of creative writing.

> You do your assignments in the lounge.

> Will you do your assignments in the lounge.

> You do your assignments in the lounge, don't you.

Will you do your assignments in the lounge?

Will you do your assignments in the lounge!

Finally, you should note that, as a rule, overpunctuating the end of a sentence should be avoided. When an abbreviation happens to be the last word in a sentence, only one period is necessary.

He planned to meet you at 2 a.m.

And when a question mark falls within a quotation mark, do *not* add a period to the end of that sentence.

Marty asked her, "How are you doing?"

Note: The end-of-the-chapter exercise on the comma also includes practice sentences involving the correct uses of terminal marks. From then on, each successive exercise may also be cumulative—that is, exercises may include punctuation marks discussed in that particular chapter, as well as punctuation marks studied up to that point.

2

The comma

The most frequently used punctuation mark, the comma, has several functions: it can signal a pause, separate thoughts or descriptions, and add an overall cadence to a sentence. Perhaps more than any other punctuation mark, the comma adds logic to whatever you are writing. Apply commas with clarity in mind so as to make the reader's flow of thought as close as possible to the meaning you intend to convey.

All chapters of this book are designed to teach you the rules about when as well as when *not* to use a certain punctuation mark. In this chapter the rules governing the use of the comma are discussed. Immediately after each rule is a set of questions that will help you to better understand its application. Following the comma rules and the exercises—and then the answers to the exercises—is a set of self-test questions as an overall practice. When you have completed the questions, check your answers against the corrected answers on pages 67, 68, and 69, as well as against the rules, until you are satisfied with what you have learned.

Rule 1

Two or more main ideas—each of which alone could be a sentence in itself—are separated by a comma when the last main idea begins with a conjunction such as *and, but, or, nor, for, so, yet, while,* and *whereas.* The comma must precede the coordinate conjunction.

He bought a new car, **and** she bought an education.

Many instructors get most of their paper work and reading done at the college, **while** others waste their time socializing in the cafeteria.

Exercise 1

Part 1: Applying Rule 1 to the following, circle the sentence or sentences that are correct:

1. The assignment may be handed in any day this week for full credit but it will be marked down 10 percent next week.
2. Mike will work the first shift, but Lucy will have to work the second shift.
3. Each student is responsible for his/her own project but, anyone may collaborate with any of the other students for further information.

Part 2: Punctuate the following sentences with commas as necessary:

1. Joe munched on a hamburger Mary fasted with a cup of tea and I indulged in a hot-fudge sundae.

2. Rosalie took turns driving the car and the truck yet she didn't give Zachary a turn.

3. I ate you are eating he will eat they will have eaten but I think we all should have been dieting.

(Answers start on page 56.)

Rule 2

No comma is used before the coordinate conjunctions *and, but, or, nor,* and *yet* when the coordinate conjunction joins two words, two phrases, or two dependent clauses. Note that in the second sentence, the second predicate uses the subject of the first predicate to form a complete statement:

> They have neither the right **nor** the ability to enforce the ethic.

> Freely, he went about his business **but** realized finally that he was developing a slight, pale countenance.

The second sentence has no comma between *business* and *but*. If there were the pronoun *he* before *realized*, then there would be a need for a comma between *business* and *but*.

Notwithstanding, reputable writers and publishers are beginning to place a comma before the coordinate conjunction in a long introductory clause even though a single subject is shared by each side of it. This comma seems unnecessary when the conjunction alone provides the necessary pausal break (see Rule 10).

> **Once you have aroused the readers' attentions, and introduced them to your product or service,** it will appear so

attractive, so necessary, and so profitable
that every reader will feel compelled to buy
or use the product or service.

⇒ *The whole opening dependent clause should
have only one comma after the word service. The reason for no comma within this opening clause is that
there are only two items in the series (Rule 11), while
the main clause has a series of three items and requires
two commas based upon the preferred Rule 10.*

Similarly, there is a tendency for writers and publishers to put a comma between the two parts of a couplet that
come after the verb in a simple sentence when the *and*
alone is sufficient.

We have agreed together **to go beyond the
limiting authorities in our own day, and to
find new authorities in our own way.**

⇒ *Rule 11 on page 38 is applicable here also.*

Exercise 2

Part 1: Applying Rule 2, circle the incorrect sentence or
sentences.

1. To be on time for every single period is not only
   a goal but also a responsibility.
2. The student did the written assignment, and
   handed it in two days before it was due.
3. The student did the written assignment, and
   she handed it in on the day it was due.

Part 2: Using what you know so far about the use of
the comma, punctuate the following:

1. You can pay now or we will bill you later.
2. The student scraped the old paint off the house on Saturday and the owner started painting it on the following Monday
3. Three days is ample time and can seem like an eternity yet it is not enough time for a vacation.
4. Fred walked to the store and bought a hot dog but he forgot to get the mustard.

Rule 3

Among the coordinate conjunctions is the word *so*; it can cause punctuation problems. If used alone, it becomes a coordinate conjunction preceded by a comma. However, if it joins the word *that* and becomes the term *so that*, then the *so that* introduces a subordinate clause with no comma.

> Sue would set the alarm on her watch for 10:45**, so** she would not forget she had to be home by eleven.

> Dance hall owners used to put sawdust on the waxed floors **so that** the dancers could more easily slide their shoes for a waltz or fox trot.

> ⇒ *The words* so *and* so that *are usually a matter of choice, but the punctuation mark is not a matter of choice.*

Exercise 3

Applying Rule 3, add the necessary punctuation to the following sentences.

1. The skit was acted out in the center of the room so that the actors and the audience could experience a theater-in-the-round performance.
2. The icy conditions are hazardous so I have decided that I should call off the 8 o'clock exercise activities.

Rule 4

One form of the use of the comma that has recently become apparent to one of the authors of this book is the use of the comma in place of the word *that*.

> The bad news is, there is one more bureaucratic hassle for small businesses. The good news is, it could in the long run save them a lot of trouble and expense.

> ⇒ *For each of the sentences in the preceding example, writers traditionally have used* that *in place of a comma, proving style of writing* does *change.*

Rule 5

Similar to the coordinate conjunctions are the correlative conjunctions *either/or, neither/nor, not only/but also, both/and.* A comma does not usually separate elements that are contrasted through the use of the pairs of coordinates.

> **Neither** our publisher **nor** I realized the error.

> Lewana was appointed to the position **not only** because she has had the experience **but also** because she has her CPA license.

Rule 6

When an introductory element—a phrase or a dependent clause, especially a lengthy one—comes before the main part of the sentence, it is followed by a comma.

> **Feeling quite content with the position he had achieved,** Jack rewarded himself with a pat on the back.

Traditionally, these introductory elements have grammatical names: adverbial clauses; participial, infinitive, absolute, or complex prepositional phrases; and adjective-cluster expressions that may either be phrasal or clausal. It is not too difficult to sense these openings before a main clause without necessarily knowing the grammatical terms.

(Note: To those students or interested readers intent on knowing more about the punctuation of introductory elements, a detailed study of the kinds of clauses and phrases explained in traditional terms appears in Chapter 15.)

Rule 7

Among the many variations of introductory styles used to open a complex or compound-complex sentence is the one in which a writer will occasionally delay a participial phrase until the noun or pronoun that the phrase modifies has been stated. Both of the following examples are acceptable sentences:

> Sara Marshall, **having gained the necessary business and computer knowledge for the printing business,** sought the position of personnel manager for Pine Island Press.

Having gained the necessary business and computer knowledge for the printing business, Sara Marshall sought the position of personnel manager for Pine Island Press.

Rule 8

A subordinate clause or phrase that *follows* a main clause (instead of preceding it) is usually not set off by a comma. For some variations and exceptions to this rule, see pages 151-152 in Chapter 12. For a list of subordinate conjunctions consult the list in the Glossary on pages 183-184.

We guarantee freshness of the product **if the product is cooked before the date stamped on the package.**

The work on the building will continue tomorrow **unless the predicted storm is too severe.**

Rule 9

No matter how short the introductory element is, if clarity or emphasis is needed, a comma is used after the introductory phrase or adverb clause to avoid misreading or to give emphasis.

As we ate, the pups sniffed around under the table for any scraps somebody might have dropped.

While they were walking, the dog broke his leash and took off onto the hot tar in full pursuit of a cat.

With little effort, he scaled the top of the huge pile of pulpwood.

Exercise 4

Part 1: Applying Rules 3 through 9, punctuate the following sentences. Those that are correct mark *C*.

1. Because the hardbound book *Ruth's Primer of Africa* cost $2,200 for all the artwork and because the indexing cost $1,100 we had to increase the retail price from $59 a book to $75 a book.

2. Walking through the woods on a brisk fall day, can provide us with many rewarding experiences.

3. Having checked all accounts receivable the clerk concluded that somebody must have given him $24 too much.

4. To achieve the highest standards possible the school committee hired the best-qualified teachers available.

5. Without any obligation order your sample record today.

Part 2: Using what you have learned up to this point, punctuate the following.

1. Having fallen asleep on the train I missed my station.

2. Consuming 14 times as many doughnuts as the rest Albert felt himself to be the champion; yet he was soon to discover the hazards of eating too much.

3. In order that we may teach a better form of punctuation we must look at the manner in which it has developed thus far.

4. On the busy street cars were jammed bumper to bumper.

5. Max must not only improve his grades but he also must organize all his artwork in a portfolio if he intends to put in an application for Rhode Island School of Design.

6. The Stop and Shop was closed for several hours because a man had mistakenly put his car in reverse and then smashed the car into the front of the store.

Rule 10

A comma is used to separate words or groups of words in a series of three or more. A comma is preferred after the next-to-the-last item so that the writer will not lead the reader to think the last two items may go together.

To get through college, he **drove a taxi days, cooked in a hash house some evenings, set up bowling pins other evenings, and fired furnaces during meal breaks.**

She **did some part-time word processing, sold sushi, and started her own freelance business** in order to save enough money for graduate school.

Some students **go to classes, take and pass tests, yet cannot maturely express the thoughts that are on their minds.**

She bought brown-and-serve rolls, **pork, and beans** to prepare an old-fashioned Saturday night supper.

The deli served rolls, **pork and beans**.

⇒ *The last two items go together in one dish.*

Most textbooks in the last 50 years have considered that it is better to include the comma after the next-to-last item—that is, before the coordinate conjunction—than trying to determine in each case whether the series may be misread without it. Admittedly, though, there are a large number of educated people who do follow and teach the style of *not* using a comma after the next-to-the-last item. Most grammarians and linguists favor the "extra comma" because the comma before the coordinate conjunction is necessary for retaining the proper pitch for each of the equal items—even for the reader who tends to hear silently what he or she reads.

The rules in English grammar, as we have all experienced, do have exceptions. (See pages 149-154 for a discussion of arbitrary uses of punctuation.) However, we must have some standards—some agreement between the writers and the readers. A writer cannot take the attitude that Humpty-Dumpty took in *Alice in Wonderland*. Remember when Alice objected, "But 'glory' doesn't mean 'a nice knockdown argument.'" And Humpty-Dumpty responded in his scornful tone, "When I use a word, it means just what I choose it to mean...." Let's not take that kind of privilege with punctuation marks!

Exercise 5

Applying what you know so far about the comma, punctuate the following sentences.

1. Cake root beer and ice cream were served to the noisy crowd of tots.

2. To celebrate the holiday we walked the dog through the thin air of early dawn prepared a breakfast of steak and eggs bathed in rose hips and tomato juice and dressed in our best clothing.

3. Betsy brought along her dolls doll house teddy bear and dump truck; Sue took along a book a comb and some aspirin; while Anthony left everything at home. (See Rule 5 on page 74 for these semicolons.)

Rule 11

Do not use a comma when there are only two items in a series, unless the two items are statements, each of which could be a sentence in itself (as Rule 1 points out).

She bought **ice cream and cake.**

A student **who works nights and who goes to school days** can burn out quickly.

Exercise 6

Applying what you have learned so far, punctuate the following sentences with commas. Mark those that are correct with a *C*.

1. He moved softly but quickly across the darkened room.

2. Five six or seven hungry people were banging slowly yet urgently upon my front door.

3. Although the two readers were similar in every other respect she enjoyed reading Plato and Aristotle whereas he liked Keats and Wordsworth.

4. In 1996 2,500 students graduated from Westfield State College with B.A. degrees.

Rule 12

When a group of words is needed within a sentence to convey the intended meaning of that sentence (rather than to add some extra information), then that group of words is not set off by commas. In grammatical terms, these groups of words are called restrictive or essential elements.

> The young man **whom Mose Carson befriended** was a tenderfoot.

> The book **(that) you are talking about** is the one **(that) I intend to read.**

⇒ *In this case,* that *is understood or implied. Almost all groups of words introduced by* that— *implied or actually stated in the sentence—are not set off by commas.*

Rule 13

A word or group of words is set off by commas when the word or group of words—commonly called an "appositive"—adds meaning to the main idea and yet is not crucial to the basic meaning.

> Sally, my neighbor, is a teacher.

However, when the word or group of words is needed to convey the intended meaning, then that word or group of words is not set off by commas.

My neighbor **Sally** is a teacher.

The previous sentence may appear to be an exception to the rule for appositives. An easy rule of thumb, even though not 100 percent accurate, is:

CAPITALIZED NOUN + common noun
= commas

common noun + CAPITALIZED NOUN
= no commas

Other examples of punctuating appositives follow:

It is acceptable to open a sentence with the **word** *and.*

Without "the **word** *and*" in this sentence, the reader would not know which word is being referred to; therefore, *and* is essential to the statement and is not set off by a comma.

She uses *and,* **a coordinate conjunction,** in every other sentence.

The term *coordinate conjunction* is additional information and, if left out, would not change the meaning of the sentence. However, the technical term does add additional information about the word *and.*

Exercise 7

Punctuate the following sentences.

1. Engrossed in the project she was working on Ms. Grossman my supervisor neglected to help me with my difficulties.

2. Our friend Clyde Binghamton found a serious problem in the program but he forgot to do all the new data entry.

It is important, at this point, to let you know that there is an exception to the use of commas: If the appositive has internal commas, strengthen the commas before and after the appositive with *dashes* in order that the eye may see the minor breaks within the major break. You will learn more about the dash later (see the section on the dash on page 88 to learn more about its appropriate uses).

1. Four employees—Greg, Terry, Glenn, and Daryl—were promoted.

2. If you have any problems with the textbook—or for that matter, with any other publication we have produced—don't hesitate to contact me.

Rule 14

This rule is similar to Rule 13 in that a word or a group of words—in this case called "nonrestrictive" or "nonessen-tial" clauses—adds meaning to the main idea and yet is not crucial to the basic meaning. Therefore, these words would also be set off by commas.

Mt. Katahdin, **brilliantly pink from the rising sun,** was a common spectacle visible from our back porch.

Aunt Mattie, **concerned about Jane's hazardous trip home through the snow storm,** dug out her snowshoes to go to meet her.

> Mose Carson, **who claimed to be Kit Carson's brother,** was always trying to make money the easy way.

> Bus 35, **which will arrive in Boston at 8:15 a.m.,** must be ready to leave for Portland at 8:30 a.m.

If the adjective clause was left out of the previous example, the meaning of the main clause would still convey the intended thought. However, the additional information about Bus 35 may help the bus dispatcher to quickly identify which incoming bus is to leave soon after its arrival in Boston. Consequently, nonrestrictive elements must provide useful or important additional information to the main idea. If this nonrestrictive material was literally "nonessential" information, it might well be superfluous.

The relative pronoun *which* introduces a nonrestrictive adjective clause. The relative pronouns *who* and *whom* may also introduce the nonrestrictive adjective clause; however, *who* and *whom* (as illustrated under Rule 12) may also introduce an essential adjective clause.

> ⇒ *Always remember that any nonrestrictive clause (or phrase) imbedded within a sentence is always set off by a pair of commas. Don't depend upon sound. Make sure you give your reader a signal to briefly pause before and then after every nonrestrictive element.*

Sometimes the writer must determine whether the clause or phrase element is restrictive or nonrestrictive. In the two following sentences the words are the same, but the punctuation makes the difference in their meanings.

> All teachers, **who shirk their responsibilities,** should be fired.

All teachers **who shirk their responsibilities**
should be fired.

The first sentence states that all teachers shirk their responsibilities and should be fired (some students feel this
way!). The second sentence states that only those who
shirk their responsibilities should be fired (many parents
feel this way!).

Furthermore, some writers appear to punctuate by
"ear," yet they, like most writers, are usually well-read. If
they are well-read, then they have become quite familiar
with the conventional system of punctuation that, with
some slight variations, has become both standardized and
recognized by our society. Consequently, these writers may
be imitating what they are in the habit of seeing.

Intonation, as the "by ear" punctuation is technically
called, cannot always be relied upon. The distinction between the restrictive and nonrestrictive elements illustrates this fact. The restrictive element identifies or limits
the meaning of the noun it refers to. Contrary to the impli-
cations of the rules found in most traditional grammar
books, the restrictive element can be left out of the sentence, and the main clause will still have meaning, but not
the intended meaning.

We will inform you about every important
development **that occurs in the legislative
meetings for the next three months.**

If the adjective clause was left out, the meaning of the
whole sentence would change because we would then "inform you about every development" whether it was in the
legislative meetings or not.

Exercise 8

Punctuate the following sentences.

1. For Mr. Newberry who is one of our best customers we have very important financial news.

2. Jill placed the package elaborately decorated with red green and blue ribbons under the tree.

3. Tipping Rock which is inaccessible by car is located in Westhampton one of the many small towns in the foothills of the Berkshires.

4. The temperature rose the atmosphere about the town hall became unbearable and the board grew tired of the apparent impasse; yet the debate overheated with the passion of its participants went on another day.

5. Employees who have liquor of any kind on their person while at work will be dismissed.

6. The word *and* and the term "you know" are overused in compositions and in speech.

Rule 15

Expressions that are imbedded within sentences or clauses are set off with commas.

> He will, **in any event,** be reviewing for the test.

> Don't you think, **off the cuff,** the purpose of his exhibition was to use us in his theory of evolution?

Palmer's snow squall was the most blinding storm I have ever heard of, and that**, I am certain,** is the reason why he was so late for class.

The commas after the word *that* set off the parenthetical expression "I am certain." However, some expressions, such as the following, are so weak that they need not be set off by commas.

Who **do you think** will be appointed editor of the school newspaper?

Exercise 9

Applying Rule 15, as well as the other rules discussed so far, place the commas where they belong in the following sentences.

1. The soil is still wet from recent rains; the farmers for that reason have not yet planted the crops.

2. Evidence of progress however slight is the objective of the course.

3. Everyone was looking for Dave the organizer of the show but he for the most part wouldn't succumb to their flattery.

Rule 16

Conjunctive adverbs of more than one syllable that are imbedded within a sentence or clause are set off with commas. (See "conjunctive adverbs" on page 175 in the Glossary.)

The exercise book, **furthermore,** shows
youths how to use weights without
overstressing their bodies.

Charles was **then** appointed chairman of the
Health Protection Advisory Board.

Rule 17

In cases when sentences are directed specifically toward someone, the person who is being addressed is set off
by a comma or commas—a pair of commas when embedded within a clause and a single comma when at the beginning or at the end of a clause.

Carl, please close the door.

See you soon, **my friend.**

To be honest, **Mack,** that is an unkind
remark.

Exercise 10

Using what you have learned so far about the use of
the comma, punctuate the following sentences.

1. Philip if you continue to torment your parents
   Stanley Marie and me all of us will have to find
   some way to discipline you.

2. I will take you the man in the black shirt for my
   team.

3. However no matter what you decide the position
   will stay open until somebody with your
   qualifications is available.

4. Our permanent home located on Pine Island Lake is a summer resort in the summer and a winter resort in the winter.

5. The basketball player short as he was could weave in and out of the opponent's defense.

Rule 18

Yes, No, and exclamations appearing at the beginning of a sentence are followed by a comma.

Yes, you have my permission.

Oh, what a marvelous day for a hayride.

Rule 19

Introductory adverbs—especially ones ending in *-ly*—and conjunctive adverbs (p. 175) are followed by a comma.

Obviously, she was not aware of your intentions.

Exercise 11

Punctuate the following:

1. Consequently Tom you must make the decision.

2. My lord the way Catherine my co-worker acted; grudgingly she made her appearance.

3. Heavens that was an exciting yet tragic film.

4. Gosh how you've grown since I last saw you.

Rule 20

Two unique uses of the comma that apply to addresses and dates (these being counterparts) are:

1. Each item after the *first* in an address or a date is set off by commas.

   Our branch office in **Portland, Maine,** was established on **June 6, 1961,** and terminated on **January 5, 1971.**

2. The comma is not used when each of the items is joined by prepositions, unless there is a comma already before or after the item.

   He moved to 555 North Main **Street in Ashby, Massachusetts, on a Monday in September of 1959.**

⇒ *There is a comma after* Massachusetts *even though there is a preposition before the following item. Because there is no preposition between* Ashby *and* Massachusetts, *commas must be used to set off the second of the two items. Remember, each item after the first is set off by commas.*

We no longer separate the month and the year with a comma. (Also see "simple prepositional phrase" in Chapter 15.)

   In **June 1996** all the building plans had the necessary financial backing.

However, when a phrase such as "In June 1996" opens a sentence, some writers prefer to follow the year with a comma. Moreover, a comma is a must when the date is followed by Arabic numbers.

In June 1996, all building plans had the necessary financial backing.

During the month of **January 1997, 230** men and women had attended one hearing or the other.

Exercise 12

Punctuate the following:

1. On Friday November 15 1994 the *S.S. Ocean Monarch* sailed from Hamilton Bermuda to New York City.

2. The Smiths moved into their new home long before its completion on August 21 1978 and moved out not a moment too soon in December of 1978.

Rule 21

Composite adjectives before nouns are not separated by commas, whereas coordinate adjectives before nouns are. To better understand these concepts, note the following two examples:

Composite adjective—

He wore **a dingy white** shirt.

⇒ *In the preceding sentence you will observe that each of the composite adjectives in turn modifies the next set of composites along with the noun— and that each does not separately modify the noun. In other words, there are no commas between a and dingy and dingy and white because a modifies* dingy white shirt, dingy *modifies* white shirt, *and* white *modifies* shirt.

Conversely, the coordinate adjectives are set off by commas, and these coordinate adjectives do—in parallel fashion—separately modify the noun.

Coordinate adjectives—

> She admired the **tall, handsome, virile lifeguard.**

> ⇒ *There are commas separating* tall *and* handsome *and* virile *because each of these adjectives is equally related to the noun* lifeguard.

There may also be a mixture of coordinates and composites in the same series.

> The **graying, wrinkled old** lady entered the room.

> ⇒ *There is a comma between* graying *and* wrinkled *because each of these words is equally modifying* old lady, *not just* lady.

Exercise 13

Punctuate the following:

1. The clerk told me that the package contained a sweet ready-to-eat oat cereal.

2. As he adjusted his partially torn gray jersey the muscular young defendant was instructed to do community service by cleaning dirty public streets.

Rule 22

A comma is used before examples introduced by *such as* or *especially*. The term *such as* may also be restrictive.

> The apartments are provided with the difficult-to-move furnishings, **such as stoves and refrigerators.**

> He likes all kinds of entertainment, **especially movies and Broadway plays.**

Rule 23

A word or part of a sentence is sometimes omitted and a comma is substituted.

> Some of the new car designs are conservative; **some, futuristic.**

> ⇒ *The second half of this sentence is an ellipsis for "some new car designs are futuristic." (See Rule 1 on page 71 for the use of semicolons.)*

Rule 24

Adjectives that follow the nouns they modify are set off by commas.

> The scraggly pine, **grotesque and barren in the cold moonlight,** leered down at the panic-stricken hikers.

If the adjectives that follow are internally punctuated with commas, then the complete series is set off by dashes.

The scraggly pine—**grotesque, barren, and cold in the moonlight**—leered down at the panic-stricken hikers.

⇒ *(See Chapter 5 for the use of dashes.)*

Rule 25

A comma is used to separate a confirmatory question from the main statement.

He ate all of his dinner, **didn't he?**

Rule 26

A comma follows the salutation of a friendly letter or a social letter and the complimentary close of any letter.

Dear Jane,

(followed by body of letter)

Sincerely yours,

(before signature at end of letter)

Rule 27

When used parenthetically, phrases of contrast and phrases of addition are set off by commas.

The duplicator is power driven, **not hand regulated.**

Persistence, **as well as courage,** is necessary
to overcome some of the obstacles of life.

Exercise 14

Punctuate the following sentences:

1. Many hearty foods are free of fat and cholesterol
   such as meat-like soy products.

2. The first show will be presented for the pre-school
   audience; the second show for grades 1 to 4.

3. The cooperating teacher showed the student
   teacher what to teach not how to teach.

4. My how you do rank amongst the tallest not to
   mention heftiest individuals to have ever
   walked this earth.

5. The scores are all registered for today are they
   not?

6. The instructor along with his most capable
   students produced a play that would match any
   off-Broadway play.

Rule 28

A comma or commas are used to separate a direct quotation from the tag *(he said, Betty commented,* etc.) unless
a period, question mark, or exclamation point is used (see
Chapter 10).

"To get full credit in English Composition
II," **the instructor stated,** "you must have
completed all compositions assigned."

⇒ *The phrase "the instructor stated" is the tag.*

Rule 29

Not too often but on some occasions, two of the same verbs will come together, in which case, place a comma between them to emphasize the meaning of each distinct verb.

> Whoever it **is, is** too late.

> The scars that the maple tree and I **have, have been** picked up in our short lives.

The first one of the two verbs ends the noun-clause subject, and the second one following it is the verb of the whole main clause.

However, if two unlike verbs appear together, a comma is not necessary.

> Whoever it **is will** be too late.

Yet don't let the two of the same verbs in a sentence like the following fool you:

> If I **had had** the book, I could have studied the assigned lesson.

In this latter example, the first verb is not the same as the second. The first *had* is a helping verb to the main verb *had*.

Exercise 15

From what you have learned from Rules 28 and 29, punctuate the following.

1. "Is it Doris Day who sang 'What will be will be'?" the little girl asked her mother.

2. "All classes will be dismissed at noon" the dean announced.

Rule 30

One comma problem is whether to set off a verb phrase that writers use very often on the end of their sentences. You may be able to determine when to set the modifier off with commas or when to position it somewhere else in the sentence by sounding out with the mind's ear the function or intended shade of meaning you wish to express in your sentence.

> The young woman went to every restaurant in the college town, **hoping that at least one of them had not already hired all the waitresses they needed.**

> The fans crowded into the stadium, **each side anticipating their team would be the winner.**

Rule 31

Commas may be used in conjunction with parentheses, brackets, ellipses, quotation marks, and periods used with abbreviations; however, commas are not used in conjunction with semicolons, colons, dashes, exclamation marks, and question marks. If you find yourself not knowing which mark to use, remember the comma is the mark that may be dropped and the other mark is retained.

"What time does the bus leave?" I asked.

"The bus leaves at 8:30 a.m.," the man told me.

Bus 35, which will arrive in Boston at 8:15 **a.m.,** must be ready to leave for Portland at 8:30 **a.m.**

⇒ *Note the comma after* 8:15 a.m. *(and the one period after* 8:30 a.m.*)*

If it doesn't stop raining in the next 24 hours—**the weather forecasters say it won't**—then we will have to partially open the gates of the dam.

⇒ *An introductory element to a main clause is followed by a comma—Rule 6; however, because of the dash no comma follows the word* won't.

The Modern Language Association recommends that in this "new system of documentation, brief parenthetical citations in [your] text refer to a bibliography at the end of [your] research **paper...,** and you may now eliminate the need for all but explanatory notes."

⇒ *A comma is used with the ellipses. Also you may like to refer to the rules for brackets later in this book.*

When you study these rules **(see page 203),** make use of all the cross references.

⇒ *Note the comma with the close parenthesis.*

Answers to the exercises

(The rules in italics, following each answer, are in the order that the commas appear within the sentence.)

Exercise 1

Part 1:

1. The assignment may be handed in any day this week for full credit, but it will be marked down 10 percent next week.
2. Mike will work the first shift, but Lucy will have to work the second shift. *Correct as is.*
3. Each student is responsible for his or her own project, but anyone may collaborate with any of the other students for further information. *Commas always precede coordinate conjunctions.*

Part 2:

1. Joc munched on a hamburger, Mary fasted with a cup of tea, and I indulged in a hot-fudge sundae. *A series of sentences (Rule 10).*
2. Rosalie took turns driving the car and the truck, yet she didn't give Zachary a turn.
3. I ate, you are eating, he will eat, they will have eaten, but I think we all should have been dieting. *A series (Rule 10).*

Exercise 2

Part 1:

1. To be on time for every single period is not only a goal but also a responsibility. *Correct as is.*
2. The student did the written assignment *[no comma]* and handed it in two days before it was due. *This sentence was incorrect—there should be no commas.*

3. The student did the written assignment, and she handed it in on the day it was due. *Correct as is.*

Part 2:

1. You can pay now, or we will bill you later.
2. The student scraped the old paint off the house on Saturday, and the owner started painting it on the following Monday.
3. Three days is ample time and can seem like an eternity, yet it is not enough time for a vacation.
4. Fred walked to the store and bought a hot dog, but he forgot to get the mustard.

Exercise 3

1. The skit was acted out in the center of the room so that the actors and the audience could experience a theater-in-the-round performance. *Correct as is—no comma.*
2. The icy conditions are hazardous, so I have decided that I should call off the 8 o'clock exercise activities. *The word* so *is coordinate.*

Exercise 4

Part 1:

1. Because the hardbound book *Ruth's Primer of Africa* cost $2,200 for all the artwork and because the indexing cost $1,100, we had to increase the retail price from $59 a book to $75 a book. *Long opening couplet opens the sentence (Rule 6).*
2. Walking through the woods on a brisk fall day *[omit comma]* can provide us with many

rewarding experiences. *Noun clause is the subject part of the whole sentence and is the subject of the verb* can provide.

3. Having checked all accounts receivable, the clerk concluded that somebody must have given him $24 too much. *The opening clause modifies the subject* clerk.

4. To achieve the highest standards possible, the school committee hired the best-qualified teachers available. *The opening phrase modifies* school committee.

5. Without any obligation, order your sample record today. *This opening phrase modifies the* you, *which is understood.*

Part 2:

1. Having fallen asleep on the train, I missed my station. *Opening phrase modifies* I.

2. Consuming 14 times as many doughnuts as the rest, Albert felt himself to be the champion; yet he was soon to discover the hazards of eating too much. *Another subordinate element preceding the main clause.*

3. In order that we may teach a better form of punctuation, we must look at the manner in which it has developed thus far. *And another introductory element (all Rule 6).*

4. On the busy street, cars were jammed bumper to bumper. *For clearness (Rule 9).*

5. Max must not only improve his grades but he also must organize all his artwork in a portfolio if he intends to put in an application for Rhode

Island School of Design. *Correct as is (Rule 5 and Rule 8).*

6. The Stop and Shop was closed for several hours because a man had mistakenly put his car in reverse and then smashed the car into the front of store. *Correct as is (Rule 8 and Rule 2).*

Exercise 5

1. Cake, root beer, and ice cream were served to the noisy crowd of tots. *(Rule 10.)*

2. To celebrate the holiday, we walked the dog through the thin air of early dawn, prepared a breakfast of steak and eggs, bathed in rose hips and tomato juice, and dressed in our best clothing. *(Rule 6 and Rule 10.)*

3. Betsy brought along her dolls, doll house, teddy bear, and dump truck; Sue took along a book, a comb, and some aspirin; while Anthony left everything at home. *(Rule 10.)*

Exercise 6

1. He moved softly but quickly across the darkened room. *Correct as is.*

2. Five, six, or seven hungry people were banging slowly yet urgently upon my front door.

3. Although the two readers were similar in every other respect, she enjoyed reading Plato and Aristotle, whereas he liked Keats and Wordsworth.

4. In 1996, 2,500 students graduated from Westfield State College with B.A. degrees.

Exercise 7

1. Engrossed in the project she was working on, Ms. Grossman, my supervisor, neglected to help me with my difficulties. (*Rule 6 and Rule 13.*)

2. Our friend Clyde Binghamton found a serious problem in the program, but he forgot to do all the new data entry. (*Rule 12 and Rule 1.*)

Exercise 8

1. For Mr. Newberry, who is one of our best customers, we have very important financial news. (*Rule 14.*)

2. Jill placed the package—elaborately decorated with red, green, and blue ribbons—under the tree. (*p. 88 and Comma Rule 10.*)

3. Tipping Rock, which is inaccessible by car, is located in Westhampton, one of the many small towns in the foothills of the Berkshires. (*Rule 14.*)

4. The temperature rose, the atmosphere about the town hall became unbearable, and the board grew tired of the apparent impasse; yet the debate, overheated with the passion of its participants, went on another day. (*Rule 10 and Rule 14. Also see Rule 4 on page 73 for semicolon before* yet.)

5. Employees who have liquor of any kind on their person while at work will be dismissed. *Correct as is.*

6. The word *and* and the term "you know" are overused in compositions and in speech. *Correct as is.*

Exercise 9

1. The soil is still wet from recent rains; the farmers, for that reason, have not yet planted the crops. (*Rule 15. See Rule 1 on page 71 for semicolon.*)

2. Evidence of progress, however slight, is the objective of the course. (*Rule 15.*)

3. Everyone was looking for Dave, the organizer of the show, but he for the most part wouldn't succumb to their flattery. *The first and second commas are based on Rule 13. The second comma, however, also plays the part of Rule 1— two rules at the same time.*

Exercise 10

1. Philip, if you continue to torment your parents, Stanley, Marie, and me, all of us will have to find some way to discipline you. *The first comma is based on Rule 17, the next three on Rule 10, and the fifth on Rule 6.*

2. I will take you, the man in the black shirt, for my team. (*Rule 17.*)

3. However, no matter what you decide, the position will stay open until somebody with your qualifications is available. (*Rule 19 and Rule 6.*)

4. Our permanent home, located on Pine Island Lake, is a summer resort in the summer and a winter resort in the winter. (*Rule 14.*)

5. The basketball player, short as he was, could weave in and out of the opponent's defense. (*Rule 14.*)

Exercise 11

1. Consequently, Tom, you must make the decision. (*Rule 19 and Rule 17.*)

2. My lord, the way Catherine, my co-worker, acted; grudgingly, she made her appearance. (*Rule 18, Rule 13, and Rule 19. Also Rule 1 on page 71 for semicolon.*)

3. Heavens, that was an exciting yet tragic film. (*Rule 18.*)

4. Gosh, how you've grown since I last saw you. (*Rule 18.*)

Exercise 12

1. On Friday, November 15, 1994, the *S.S. Ocean Monarch* sailed from Hamilton, Bermuda, to New York City.(*#1 under Rule 20. See italics rule on pages 121-122.*)

2. The Smiths moved into their new home long before its completion on August 21, 1978, and moved out not a moment too soon in December of 1978. (*#1 and #2 under Rule 20 in that order. For plural of* Smith, *see pages 133-134.*)

Exercise 13

1. The clerk told me that the package contained a sweet, ready-to-eat oat cereal. (*Rule 21) Here* sweet *and* ready-to-eat *are coordinates and* oat *is a composite. Remember that even with coordinate adjectives no comma will appear after the final adjective or before the noun that the series of adjectives modify.*

2. As he adjusted his partially torn gray jersey, the muscular, young defendant was instructed to do community service by cleaning dirty public streets. *(Rule 6 and Rule 21) As in the previous example, the complication of the difference between coordinate adjectives and composite adjectives in this sentence needs some serious study and observation.*

Exercise 14

1. Many hearty foods are free of fat and cholesterol, such as meat-like soy products. *(Rule 22.)*

2. The first show will be presented for the pre-school audience; the second show, for grades 1 to 4. *(Rule 23.)*

3. The cooperating teacher showed the student teacher what to teach, not how to teach. *(Rule 27.)*

4. My, how you do rank amongst the tallest, not to mention heftiest, individuals to have ever walked this earth. *(Rule 18 and Rule 15 or 27.)*

5. The scores are all registered for today, are they not? *(Rule 25.)*

6. The instructor, along with his most capable students, produced a play that would match any off-Broadway play. *(Rule 27.)*

Exercise 15

1. "Is it Doris Day who sang, 'What will be, will be'?" the little girl asked her mother. *(Rule 28 and Rule 29.)*

2. "All classes will be dismissed at noon," the dean announced. *(Rule 28.)*

Practice exercise

Insert punctuation marks where needed in each of the following sentences. In the blanks to the left, indicate the rule number or numbers for each of the commas you insert. If the end mark should be something other than a period, write that mark in over the period. One sentence is correct. Mark it *C*.

_____ 1. The author asked me how I made the attractive marbled cover for her book.

_____ 2. Audi my wife's dog thinks he owns all the land on our side of the lake while our cat is the king rodent catcher.

_____ 3. Kermit's body thin and bright green seems fragile to look at yet his voice is boisterous and sometimes overbearing.

_____ 4. Robin admires Kermit his friends look up to him for his leadership qualities and Miss Piggy adores him.

_____ 5. Although both Kermit and Miss Piggy are related there are also several distinct differences such as their physical appearances their personalities and their attitudes.

_____ 6. Miss Piggy who is considered by most to be the star contributes to the success of the show.

_____ 7. Computers moreover play a vital role in all businesses and at the same time encourage new and fascinating approaches to the various fields of education.

_____ 8. Jerry a student in my Fundamentals of Writing course informed me that she could

not find the word *mnemonic* in her pocket
dictionary.

_____ 9. Although most of the one hundred or so
members of my family are dyslexic the
majority of them have learned to read
rapidly and comprehensively.

_____ 10. The Japanese-style bridge which Todd
designed constructed and placed over the
small brook in our back yard is a work of
art.

_____ 11. Officer can you direct me toward the
Southeast Expressway.

_____ 12. Oh How ornate Did your architect plan for
the design to look like that.

_____ 13. You organized the party so that everyone
would have a partner didn't you.

_____ 14. The Barnum and Bailey Circus the
greatest three-ring show on earth will be
coming to town on May 5 1997 so I will
have to gather up all the grandchildren for
that occasion.

_____ 15. The show will move into Springfield
Massachusetts at about 8 p.m. Saturday
May 4 1997 for this gala event.

_____ 16. Ethel certain that she could be at least
runner up in the speaking contest
practiced in front of her mother and father
in front of her brothers and sisters and in
front of her neighbors.

_____ 17. For your information on the first of the
month your bill will be mailed to you
unless you decide to come to the office and
pick it up.

_____ 18. From September 1940 to June 1941 I studied ancient Greek a most difficult-to-learn language.

_____ 19. Some college courses consist of new and exciting information; others the most boring information.

_____ 20. We go grocery shopping intending to buy only a few items; however we always end up buying more than we expected to not because we needed them but because we bumped into them in one of the aisles.

_____ 21. Why do you think he would get up at 5 a.m.

_____ 22. Yes what the true meaning of his message is is anybody's guess.

Answers to practice exercise

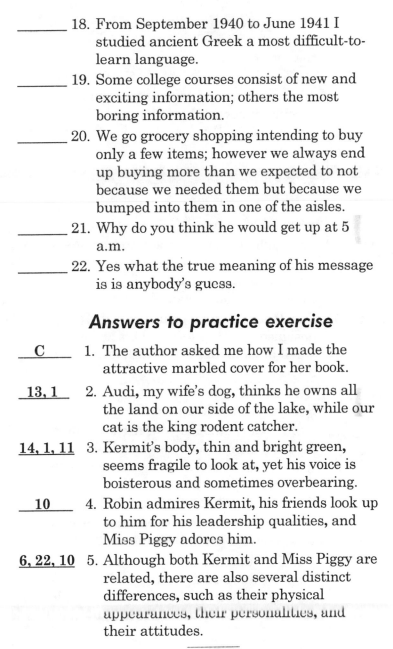

__C__ 1. The author asked me how I made the attractive marbled cover for her book.

__13, 1__ 2. Audi, my wife's dog, thinks he owns all the land on our side of the lake, while our cat is the king rodent catcher.

__14, 1, 11__ 3. Kermit's body, thin and bright green, seems fragile to look at, yet his voice is boisterous and sometimes overbearing.

__10__ 4. Robin admires Kermit, his friends look up to him for his leadership qualities, and Miss Piggy adores him.

__6, 22, 10__ 5. Although both Kermit and Miss Piggy are related, there are also several distinct differences, such as their physical appearances, their personalities, and their attitudes.

__14__   6. Miss Piggy, who is considered by most to be the star, contributes to the success of the show.

__16, 2__   7. Computers, moreover, play a vital role in all businesses and at the same time encourage new and fascinating approaches to the various fields of education.

__13__   8. Jerry, a student in my Fundamentals of Writing course, informed me that she could not find the word *mnemonic* in her pocket dictionary.

__6, 11__   9. Although most of the one hundred or so members of my family are dyslexic, the majority of them have learned to read rapidly and comprehensively.

__14, 10__   10. The Japanese-style bridge, which Todd designed, constructed, and placed over the small brook in our back yard, is a work of art.

__17__   11. Officer, can you direct me toward the Southeast Expressway?

_____   12. Oh! How ornate! Did your architect plan for the design to look like that? *No commas unless you chose to write:* Oh, **h**ow ornate! Did your architect plan for the design to look like that?

__3, 25__   13. You organized the party so that everyone would have a partner, didn't you?

__13, 20, 1__   14. The Barnum and Bailey Circus, the greatest three-ring show on earth, will be coming to town on May 5, 1997, so I will have to gather up all the grandchildren for that occasion. *The comma after* 1997 *serves two purposes. (Rule 20 and Rule 1.)*

__20 #1__ 15. The show will move into Springfield, Massachusetts, at about 8 p.m., Saturday, May 4, 1997, for this gala event.

__7, 10__ 16. Ethel, certain that she could be at least runner up in the speaking contest, practiced in front of her mother and father, in front of her brothers and sisters, and in front of her neighbors.

__9, 8, 11__ 17. For your information, on the first of the month your bill will be mailed to you unless you decide to come to the office and pick it up.

__20 #2,__
__6, 13__ 18. From September 1940 to June 1941, I studied ancient Greek, a most difficult-to-learn language.

__11, 23__ 19. Some college courses consist of new and exciting information; others, the most boring information.

__30, 19,__
__27, 2__ 20. We go grocery shopping, intending to buy only a few items; however, we always end up buying more than we expected to, not because we needed them but because we bumped into them in one of the aisles.

__15__ 21. Why, do you think, he would get up at 5 a.m.?

__18, 29__ 22. Yes, what the true meaning of his message is, is anybody's guess.

3

The semicolon

The semicolon is used specifically to coordinate elements of equal rank. Of this punctuation mark, there are five uses; any attempt to use the semicolon in any other manner is incorrect. Keep in mind that whenever using the semicolon, a particular structure on one side of it must be balanced by an equal element on the other side. This requirement will become more apparent in Rule 5 where the two sides are shown to be even more clinically related.

The semicolon is one of the most confusing and least understood elements of punctuation. Many students confuse it with the colon. Whereas the colon (:) is directed at something that is to follow, the semicolon (;) acts as a fulcrum, balancing two elements of the same kind of structure.

Please note that not just any two statements can be joined together in this way; there must be a logical linking of sentences for the semicolon to have its proper effect. It is almost as though it were a symbol of relationships—a catalyst, perhaps—between complete clauses. Because of the popularity of terse sentences today, the semicolon between two independent clauses is giving way to what formerly were unpopular structures:

1. The semicolon is giving way to a period between the two independent clauses, making two sentences instead of one compound sentence.

2. The comma and the coordinate conjunction is giving way also to the period even if the second clause becomes a sentence beginning with *and, but,* or even *or.*

Bear in mind, however, that separating two independent clauses with a comma—and no coordinate conjunction—is still a comma splice or comma fault.

Following this section is a quiz consisting of seven practice sentences that test you on the use of the semicolon, as well as the comma. Use this practice to more fully understand the uses of these two punctuation marks. Your own writing will show the better for it.

Rule 1

The semicolon is used to join two main ideas (each of which alone could be a sentence in itself) when the second main idea does *not* begin with *and, but, or, nor, for, so, yet, while,* and *whereas.*

> Some people enjoy staying home during vacations; others prefer to spend this time as far away from home as possible.

Rule 2

A semicolon is used to join two main ideas (each of which alone could be a sentence in itself) joined by a conjunctive adverb. A comma follows the conjunctive adverb when it has two syllables or more—with the exception of the word *also* (see the "Glossary" for a list of conjunctive adverbs).

> The reservoir is down 35 feet; **consequently,**
> we are not permitted to water our lawns.

Conjunctive adverbs, like most adverbs that modify verbs, are versatile. This freedom allows the writer to move an adverb such as *however* from one position to another and still maintain its effectiveness within the sentence. To illustrate this flexibility, the conjunctive adverb *however* plays several different roles in the following examples. No wonder so many people become confused about punctuating this word!

> We will accept your manuscript
> in February; **however,** we would have
> preferred to have had it in December.

> We will accept your manuscript in
> February; **we would, however,** have
> preferred to have had it in December.
> ⇒ *Same as previous example but embedded within the second of two main clauses.*

The placement of *however* in the following example is usually awkward and thus rarely used; however, it does show a variation in semicolon Rule 2, with the comma preceding the conjunctive adverb and the semicolon following it.

> All encryption can be broken, **however;** and
> the work required to break the code depends
> largely on the length of the key.

Rule 3

A semicolon is used to join two main ideas when the second main idea functions to explain the first. Such sentences often use the words: *that is, in other words, for example,* or *for instance.*

> Extra accessories are available; **for example,**
> a windshield-washer unit and back-up lights
> are included.

⇒ *The second part of this compound sentence could stand alone as a sentence by itself.*

When these explanatory terms appear before a second sentence-like main clause to illustrate the first main clause, they are punctuated in the same manner as conjunctive adverbs between two main clauses. You will see in the study of the dash, when the second element is a word, a phrase, or a dependent clause—not an independent clause—a dash is used (see explanation and examples on pages 88-89 in Chapter 5.

> Extra accessories are available—**for example,**
> **fog lights and cruise control.**

⇒ *The part following the explanatory term cannot stand alone as a sentence as can the second part of the previous example.*

Rule 4

In a situation where two main ideas are joined by *and, but, or, nor, for, so, yet, while,* and *whereas* and when either or both of the two main ideas have internal commas, a semicolon can be used in place of the comma before the coordinate conjunction in an effort to strengthen and clarify the major and minor (or subordinate) parts of the concept.

> The contract is ready for our signatures; **and if our terms are agreeable,** we will meet and exchange signatures.

Note that because a comma is used after the word *agreeable*, a semicolon—not a comma—is used before the coordinate conjunction. Because of the presence of the internal comma after the word *agreeable*, the semicolon tends to strengthen what would normally be a comma before the *and*. However, many writers prefer the weaker mark, the comma, before the coordinate conjunction even though there are other internal commas.

To avoid this problem of whether to use a comma or a semicolon before the coordinate conjunction, you should consider rewriting the second of the two independent clauses by beginning it with one of the conjunctive adverbs listed on page 175. For example, the conjunctive adverb *moreover* could replace the coordinate conjunction *and, however* could replace *but*, etc.—with the proper punctuation, of course. (Refer to Rule 2.)

Rule 5

The semicolon is also used to join each word or groups of words in a series when those elements already have internal commas.

> **Mary, the tailor; Lloyd, the seamstress; and Rosey, the riveter,** comprised the threesome representing different trades at the conference.
>
> ⇒ *After the word* riveter *there is not another grouping; therefore, the appositive is simply set off by commas.*

Send examination copies of your books to our
distributors in **Hartford, Connecticut;
Bangor, Maine; and Easthampton,
Massachusetts.**

To get an A or a B on your term paper,
Research Papers, Step-by-Step recommends the
following procedure: **first, search through
the sources available to you and jot down
direct quotations and paraphrases pertinent
to your chosen topic; second, eventually set
aside your documented materials and write
a rough draft; third, integrate the
appropriate quotations and paraphrases into
your rough draft; and finally, polish up the
rough draft with the proper documentation
into a presentable final copy.**

Some writers—those who are not familiar with the five
basic uses of the semicolon—are inclined to misuse the
semicolon in the following sentence structures. (Note: The
correct punctuation is used here in place of an incorrect
semicolon.)

1. Introduce a list with a colon.

   The grocery list his wife gave him was a menu
   for breakfast: bacon, eggs, bread, milk, butter,
   and coffee.

2. Separate a subordinate element from the main
   clause with a comma.

   Because waking up every morning five days
   a week year round to the same routine
   seemed as if it would be a lifetime of
   boredom, Frank decided he would go into
   business for himself.

3. Separate a nonrestrictive or an appositive element from the element that it renames or refers to with a comma.

Your custom-made windows, which you intend to install in the room with the hot tub, will have to be back-ordered.

With the exception of Rule 5, most writers prefer to use periods in place of semicolons. However, the semicolon is still a valuable mark of punctuation, and the correct use of it can enhance the readability and clarity of any written work.

Practice exercise

Applying what you have learned in the three preceding sections, insert the correct punctuation marks where needed. For each semicolon used, write 1, 2, 3, 4, or 5 next to the sentence to indicate which of the five rules were applicable. If the end mark should be other than a period, write that mark in over the period.

_____ 1. The soil is still wet from recent rains for that reason the farmers have not yet planted the crop.

_____ 2. It appeared to be a get-together for the would-be teachers however it turned out to be an entertaining sneak preview of a new educational computer program.

_____ 3. The officer at the gate will want to know who you are but if you show him this pass card he will wave you through.

_____ 4. Todd and Toni live in Amherst Massachusetts Todd's cousins somewhere in the central part of Maine.

_____ 5. Linda Flower author of *Problem Solving Strategies in Writing* Martha Koln author of *Understanding English Grammar* and Elizabeth McMahan co-author of *The Writer's Rhetoric* are among some of the most recent female writers whose innovative approaches have added a touch of excitement to some of the normally boring English grammar books.

_____ 6. Ladies and gentlemen Governor Wilson will join our council at 11 a.m. in fact he has already met with some members at the YWCA.

_____ 7. All appliances should be turned off before you leave the house for example be sure you don't leave the clothes dryer running.

Answers to practice exercise

__1__ 1. The soil is still wet from recent rains; for that reason, the farmers have not yet planted the crop.

__2__ 2. It appeared to be a get-together for the would-be teachers; however, it turned out to be an entertaining sneak preview of a new educational computer program.

__4__ 3. The officer at the gate will want to know who you are; but if you show him this pass card, he will wave you through. *A comma is not needed after* but *so that the eye can move smoothly from the major break (;) to the minor break (,) after* card.

__1__ 4 Todd and Toni live in Amherst, Massachusetts; Todd's cousins, somewhere in the central part of Maine. *The comma after the word* cousins *is based on Rule 23 in Chapter 2.*

___5___ 5. Linda Flower, author of *Problem Solving Strategies in Writing;* Martha Koln, author of *Understanding English Grammar;* and Elizabeth McMahan, co-author of *The Writer's Rhetoric,* are among some of the most recent female writers whose innovative approaches have added a touch of excitement to some of the normally boring English grammar books. *Remember the last item—with* McMahan—*is set off by commas as an appositive; and because it is the last item in the series, a comma, not a semicolon, is needed after the word* rhetoric.

___2___ 6. Ladies and gentlemen, Governor Wilson will join our council at 11 a.m.; in fact, he has already met with some members at the YWCA.

___3___ 7. All appliances should be turned off before you leave the house; for example, be sure you don't leave the clothes dryer running.

4

The colon

The colon—perhaps more so than any other punctuation mark—gives further emphasis to what has already been said and calls attention to what is to follow an opening statement. It may introduce words, phrases, clauses, or any combination or series of these.

The functions of the colon are:

1. It signals the special relationship between the part before the colon and the part following the colon by clarifying, defining, or emphasizing the opening of the sentence.

   A foreign diplomat needs three special qualities: wisdom, tact, and knowledge.

   The athlete had only one outstanding strength: He had great speed.

   Every man and woman has three aims: to live, to love, to learn.

   The reason for my deficiency in writing can be summarized in one word: neglect.

2. It introduces a list (often the words *following* or *as follows* indicate a list, and a colon should be used).

   Materials being mailed to your store consist of the **following** items: a camera, a projector, and six films.

3. It introduces a formal or a long quotation with such words as *reads* or *read* and *writes* or *write*.

   Wordsworth **wrote** of Keats: "The calibre of such a man is mitigated by his ostentatious attitude."

4. It is used after introductory labels.

   A word of caution: Keep this synthetic material away from heat and flame.

5. It introduces subtitles of a book or other titled items.

   Punctuation: A Rationale of American Practices

6. It introduces the body of a business letter.

   Dear Editor:

   Your request for...

7. It may be used to separate—rather than to anticipate—information.

   a) chapter and verse:

   John 8:1-15

b) act and scene:

To Have and To Hold, **Act Three: Scene One**

c) hour and minute:

8:30 a.m.

d) volume and page reference:

Britannica, **14:795**

e) city of publication and the publisher in a bibliography:

New York: Macmillan

f) parts of comparison with double colon between pairs:

40:20::80:40

g) analogy:

topic sentence : paragraph :: theme : essay :: theses : dissertation

Many people confuse the semicolon (;) with the colon (:) and vice versa. The period can be substituted for the semicolon, whereas a dash may be substituted for a colon. The colon cannot be used a) to separate a preposition and its object or objects, b) to separate a verb and its object or objects, or c) to separate *for example, such as, that is, including,* etc., from the words that these explanatory terms introduce. The following examples are correct, but the places where erroneous uses of colons sometimes occur are noted.

She returned with [*misuse of colon occurs here*]
a freshly caught trout, a can of worms, and a
bouquet of wild flowers.

The items included in Lilly's knapsack were
[*misuse of colon occurs here*] an umbrella, a
new pair of sneakers, and a bouquet of wild
flowers.

The writer of the research paper ignored the
1995 MLA style completely; he used old
footnote terms such as [*misuse of colon occurs
here*] *ibid., op. cit.,* and *loc. cit.*

Note: Keep punctuation marks at a minimum; and
when more than one punctuation mark must be used si-
multaneously with another, they are placed in a logical
pattern.

Please have the following supplies in my
office by **10 a.m.**: 10 reams of 60-pound
white paper, one box of 3/8 size plastic
combs, and two boxes of covers.

⇒ *Notice that the abbreviation dot after the* m *is
retained, and it precedes the colon.*

Practice exercise

Applying what you have learned in the four chapters
on the terminal marks, the comma, the semicolon, and
now on the colon, punctuate the following sentences with
those marks you consider appropriate.

1. The directions for removing all the double spaces
   after the terminal marks and replacing them
   with single spaces are as follows Select "Edit" on

your computer and go to "Find." "Find" will say "Find What." Hit the space bar twice. Then click on "Replace." Up will come "Replace With." In the lower blank bar, hit the space key *once.* Click on "Replace All." A comment will appear showing you how many unnecessary double spaces have been eliminated. Click on "Close" and all double spaces at the end of all sentences have been replaced with single spaces.

2. A sign at Ocean City reads "Boats for Hire Here from 8 30 a.m. until 4 00 p.m."

3. It is with great pleasure that I present our guest speaker for the evening George Chartier a magician who in my opinion outperforms all the recorded Houdini tricks.

4. The book *Research Paper Step-by-Step Simplified Method of Learning the Research Process* is not only a workbook but also a textbook.

5. Dear Dr. Brown

   Enclosed along with my medical records from Dr. Morey is a recent blood profile. Will you interpret the meanings of the following items in the profile list HDL, LDL blood glucose and triglycerides

   Sincerely

   Sarah Franklin

6. While living at the Katahdin Nursing Home my mother enjoyed such events as sing-alongs ceramics religious services and handicraft exhibits.

Answers to practice exercise

1. The directions for removing all the double spaces after the terminal marks and replacing them with single spaces are as follows: Select "Edit" on your computer and go to "Find." "Find" will say, "Find What." Hit the space bar twice. Then click on "Replace." Up will come "Replace With." In the lower blank bar, hit the space key *once.* Click on "Replace All." A comment will appear showing you how many unnecessary double spaces have been eliminated. Click on "Close," and all double spaces at the end of all sentences have been replaced with single spaces.

2. A sign at Ocean City reads: "Boats for Hire Here from 8:30 a.m. until 4:00 p.m."

3. It is with great pleasure that I present our guest speaker for the evening: George Chartier, a magician who, in my opinion, outperforms all the recorded Houdini tricks.

4. The book *Research Paper, Step-by-Step: Simplified Method of Learning the Research Process* is not only a workbook but also a textbook. *A dash could be used in place of the colon.*

5. Dear Dr. Brown:

   Enclosed, along with my medical records from Dr. Morey, is a recent blood profile. Will you interpret the meanings of the following items in the profile list: HDL, LDL, blood glucose, and triglycerides?

   Sincerely,

   Sarah Franklin

6. While living in the Katahdin Nursing Home, my mother enjoyed such events as sing-alongs, ceramics, religious services, and handicraft exhibits.

5

The dash

As unique as the colon is, it has limits the dash does not have—that is, the thought beginning after the colon must eventually finish the sentence. Unlike the colon, the dash allows the writer to introduce words, phrases, and clauses into a sentence and move back into the main clause.

Dash:

> part of main idea—related thought—back into main idea

Colon:

> all of main idea: related idea introduced by main idea [period]

In the following sentence, the writer could choose a dash in place of the colon.

> The opening of his thesis has one purpose—and one purpose only: to convince smokers that tobacco controls every precious second of their lives.

Like the comma—but unlike the semicolon and colon—the dash may be used either singularly or in pairs, depending upon the position of the element it punctuates in the sentence. Traditionally, the dash was produced by two consecutive hyphens (*en dashes*) on a typewriter and one solid line that would equal the length of two hyphens when handwritten or typeset. Today, however, even though one may still produce a dash with two hyphens on a computer, it is preferable to make an *em dash*—an element that can be created or pulled up on word-processing programs. (Note its use throughout this very paragraph.)

In this section, we have used some impromptu exercises rather than specific sets of questions to illustrate more fully the concepts projected. Again, please use these to better understand the functions of the dash. Also note that the dash has related uses; that is, there are situations where sentences containing dashes could be punctuated with other marks. This makes the dash a useful tool in the quest for clarity—as all punctuation marks are.

Along with keeping punctuation at a minimum and in a logical pattern is the necessity to use correct spacing. For example, the *em dash* (—) and the *en dash* (-) or hyphen have no spaces before or after them. Look carefully at the examples in this chapter.

Appositive

A statement may act as an appositive to a word or name within a sentence. To tie it in closely with the main idea, the writer sets the appositive sentence into the main sentence by punctuating the appositive sentence with dashes.

Professor Yuan—**he is one of our most conscientious instructors**—fills the

chalkboard with lecture notes pertaining to
the succeeding lecture.

In the foregoing sentence, the appositive could also be
a sentence of its own if it appeared alone after the main
part of the sentence—that is, after the final word *lecture.*
Granted, this sentence could substitute parentheses for
the dashes, but the difference is a matter of tone and emphasis. We will learn about parentheses in the next chapter.

Explanatory material

Explanatory words, phrases, and dependent clauses
(not independent clauses)—introduced by *for example, that
is, in other words, for instance, namely,* and the sometimes
nonrestrictive *such as*—are set off by dashes. Because each
of these terms may introduce elements with internal
commas, the break before the explanatory term must be indicated by a stronger mark than a mere comma. The only
strong mark available in this instance is the dash. As you
may recall, the semicolon sets off *independent* clauses introduced by these explanatory terms (refer to Chapter 3).

> All the necessary components—**for example,
> transparencies, program guide, student
> manual, answer key, and viewing stage**—
> will be included in your teaching unit.

The preceding sentence could also be written:

> All necessary components will be included in
> your teaching unit—**for example,
> transparencies, program guide, student
> manual, answer key, and viewing stage.**

The words that follow *for example* are not a complete
sentence; therefore, the dash is used.

> Other essential parts—**such as the glossary
> and the index**—aid the student as he studies
> the content of a textbook.

Because there are no internal marks in this nonrestrictive
element, commas may be preferred in place of dashes. A
dash may be used to add further explanation or emphasis.

> **The tree that I think looks most like me is
> a young maple in my yard—*a maple that is
> just beginning to grow and take on some
> shape.***

Exercise 1

Considering the relationships just discussed, punctuate the following sentence with dashes and commas where
they most logically belong.

1. Other essential parts such as the table of
   contents or outline the glossary and the index
   aid the student as he or she studies the content
   of a textbook.

Note the punctuation of the explanatory term *such as*
when used restrictively:

> Behavior **such as this** requires strong
> disciplinary measures.

Because the term *such as this* is dependent upon the
word *behavior* for its meaning, neither the dash nor any
other form of punctuation is used.

For variety and effect, a series that explains the main
clause may appear before the main part of the sentence,
creating in the reader a feeling of anticipation. When this
series precedes the noun or pronoun to which it refers, a

dash is used to separate it from the summarizing remark that follows.

> **Studying the assigned lesson thoroughly, doing research on the subject, and preparing a detailed lesson plan**—all these are essential preliminaries for effective teaching.

Before there were specific uses for the dash, a sentence of this type would have been written:

> All these are essential preliminaries for effective teaching: studying the assigned lesson thoroughly, doing research on the subject, and preparing a detailed lesson plan.

Clarification of indefinite references

Too often in the context of writing, the writer uses a *that* that refers to a vague antecedent.

> Our bodies go through voluntary responses or anxiety reactions increasing our blood pressure, heart rate, breathing rate, and blood circulation to the muscles **that** prepare us for conflict or escape.

Traditionally, the relative pronoun *that*—like the relative pronouns *who* and *which*—has as an antecedent the noun or pronoun immediately preceding it. If the *that* is referring to the idea in the preceding phrase or phrases and not an immediately preceding noun or pronoun, the writer should use a dash and a word or words echoing the idea that the *that* is referring to. In the above sentence, because *that* refers to more than *muscles*, an echo term

must be used to pick up the complete idea preceding the
that:

> Our bodies go through voluntary responses
> or anxiety reactions increasing our blood
> pressure, heart rate, breathing rate, and
> blood circulation to the muscles—**a bodily
> process that prepares us for conflict or
> escape.**

⇒ *The phrase "a bodily process" is the specific
echo term.*

To clarify a possible misreading—one less serious than
the previous example—is the following example where, if
the reader stops to think, he or she will realize that the
antecedent of *that* is *business*, not *model*. Avoid the possibility of ambiguity by using a dash and repeating the specific word referred to.

Acceptable:

> Roy Miller, owner of Miller Printing
> Company on State Street, is exhibiting a
> model made by his business **that has come
> back from the brink of bankruptcy.**

Clearer and more emphasis:

> Roy Miller, owner of Miller Printing
> Company on State Street, is exhibiting a
> model made by his business—**a business that
> has come back from the brink of
> bankruptcy.**

⇒ *The echo word is* business. *Even though repetition often is unnecessary, it is just as often necessary for emphasis.*

Series

A series appearing at the end of a statement may be followed by another supporting remark or afterthought related to the series. It also is introduced by a dash.

Exercise 2

Without having seen a similar example of this use of the dash, try your skill on the following sentence by placing the dash and the commas in the correct place.

1. Our program will bolster your skills in higher mathematics vocabulary reading comprehension English logic analogies all the subjects heavily weighted on the Scholastic Aptitude Test and other college entrance examinations.

Emphasis

Occasionally, the dash can be used to set off a remark in order to call attention to what the writer wants to emphasize or de-emphasize in a statement.

> For variety—**and especially for effect**—a series may appear before the main part of the sentence and create a mounting climax.

Exercise 3

Punctuate the following sentence with dashes.

1. Like the comma but unlike the semicolon and the colon the dash may be used either singularly or in pairs.

Interruption

A dash may also indicate a break, a shift, or an interruption in thought.

In addition to keeping your car cool, an air conditioner permits the windows to be closed, thus avoiding wind noises. An air conditioner also—**well, let's let our dealer demonstrate for you its many advantages.**

When written, this seems to be an incorrect sentence. Try reading this sentence aloud, with a break where the dash occurs. In fact, it makes sense in the right context.

Introduction

A dash, instead of a colon, is often used to introduce words or phrases.

He had one great weakness—**a tendency to be garrulous.**

He was a successful teacher because he had developed a simple characteristic—**enthusiasm.**

It is with great pleasure that I present our guest speaker for the evening—**Mr. James Buxham.**

The following always participate—**Susan, Mary Anne, and Hope.**

The athlete had only one outstanding strength—**he had great speed.**

Credits

A dash may be used to give credit to a quotation. In this function it is placed before the name of the author.

An honest man's the noblest work of God.

—**Alexander Pope**

An honest God is the noblest work of man.

—**Samuel Butler**

Technical notes

In the following sentence, the second dash supersedes the comma, which would normally be used at the end of a long introductory element. The information contained within the pairs of dashes serves to make the separation in the sentence in the same manner that the comma would.

> **If you read each of your sentences objectively—that is, as though you are the reader rather than the writer—**you will tend to punctuate for clarity.

The dash may supersede the comma, but the semicolon supersedes the dash as illustrated in the following sentence:

> **The nonrestrictive element is set off by commas—and sometimes by dashes;** the restrictive element is not punctuated.

Like the semicolon, dashes are used to strengthen the organization of the sentence when an appositive phrase has internal commas. Using this technique, the following sentence is more elaborately constructed.

> Efficient textbook study procedures—
> **previewing the general format of the lesson, scanning all the paragraphs for key**

ideas, and close-study reading for significant data—all contribute to a student's success in college.

Exercise 4

Punctuate the following sentences with commas, semicolons, colons, and dashes.

1. All four characters Hindley Catherine Heathcliff and Edgar play vital roles in the development of Emily Brontë's novel *Wuthering Heights*.

2. Dig a hole a little larger than the spread of the roots fill the hole with water until it overflows remove the burlap wrapped around the roots gently position the tree into the prepared hole and complete the planting by packing rich soil in and around the roots these are the steps for planting small evergreen trees.

3. *Vary the structure of the preceding sentence by reversing the sentence order:* These are the steps for planting small evergreen trees... *(Finish the sentence with the series of steps listed in the preceding sentence.)*

4. A number of trees are available for landscaping your property maple birch and oak however for a fast-growing tree choose one of the many varieties of evergreens.

5. Most evergreens for instance spruce hemlock fir and balsam fir will easily grow in the upper two-thirds of the U.S. still spruce and fir are native to only the most northern regions.

6. Will was well-groomed for the wedding tuxedo ruffled shirt bow tie and patent leather shoes.

The dash may seem arbitrary—and to a degree it is—because in some sentences it is interchangeable with the colon, in others, with parentheses, and in still others, with the comma. However, the colon is used singly and can appear only before an element ending the sentence. Parentheses, which can be used only in pairs, are more interchangeable with the dash, *except that parentheses convey ideas more remotely related to the sentence.* Moreover, there are certain instances when nothing but the dash can be used—with internally punctuated appositives, with explanatory elements, and with a series that is inverted to appear at the opening of the sentence.

Answers to the exercises

Exercise 1

1. Other essential parts—such as the table of contents or outline, the glossary, and the index—aid the student as he or she studies the content of a textbook.

Exercise 2

1. Our program will bolster your skills in higher mathematics, vocabulary, reading comprehension, English, logic, analogies—all the subjects heavily weighted on the Scholastic Aptitude Test and other college entrance examinations.

Exercise 3

1. Like the comma—but unlike the semicolon and the colon—the dash may be used either singularly or in pairs.

Exercise 4

1. All four characters—Hindley, Catherine, Heathcliff, and Edgar—play vital roles in the development of Emily Brontë's novel *Wuthering Heights.*

2. Dig a hole a little larger than the spread of the roots, fill the hole with water until it overflows, remove the burlap wrapped around the roots, gently position the tree into the prepared hole, and complete the planting by packing rich soil in and around the roots—these are the steps for planting small evergreen trees.

3. These are the steps for planting small evergreen trees: Dig a hole a little larger than the spread of the roots, fill the hole with water until it overflows, remove the burlap wrapped around the roots, gently position the tree into the prepared hole, and complete the planting by packing rich soil in and around the roots.

4. A number of trees are available for landscaping your property—maple, birch, and oak; however, for a fast-growing tree, choose one of the many varieties of evergreens.

5. Most evergreens—for instance, spruce, hemlock, fir, and balsam fir—will easily grow in the upper two-thirds of the U.S.; still spruce and fir are native to only the most northern regions.

6. Will was well-groomed for the wedding—tuxedo, ruffled shirt, bow tie, and patent-leather shoes.

or

Will was well-groomed for the wedding: tuxedo, ruffled shirt, bow tie, patent-leather shoes.

6

Parentheses and brackets

Compared to a punctuation mark as often used as the comma, both parentheses (parenthesis, singular) and brackets (sometimes called "square brackets") are very limited in their respective uses. Having similar or parallel functions, the two seem alike; yet the two marks have very specific uses and cannot be interchanged.

Parentheses

Parentheses are, first of all, used to set off material that the writer feels important enough to mention but not directly related to the idea in the context where it appears. Seemingly, pairs of commas or dashes function in the same manner as the parentheses, yet materials set off by parentheses tend to be more remote to the purpose of the sentence than the information commonly set off by commas or dashes. The exact difference is a matter of importance, thus up to the writer's discretion. We can state that these remote ideas are generally cross-references, explanations, illustrations, or definitions; yet they are not absolutes.

Side remark:

> Miss Celia Kelley **(she handles all our accounts)** can assist you with this financial transaction.

Appositive:

> The dash **(a mark so overworked by the beginning writer)** impresses the reader when it has been expertly used.

The most common use of parentheses is to indicate a cross-reference.

> Summey, in his book *American Punctuation,* considers paragraphing as a kind of punctuation **(see page 17).**

Particularly important, since the discontinuance of the documentary footnotes in writing a research paper using the MLA style, is the parenthetical reference at the end of a quotation or paraphrase giving credit to the source in the bibliographic listing.

> Stephen Hawking compares the event horizon to "what Dante said of the entrance to Hell: 'All hope abandon, ye who enter here'" **(89).**

⇒ *Also note uses of quotation marks, to be discussed later.*

> ...black holes do emit radiation that is too small to be detected with today's technology **(Arny 408).**

The parentheses also enclose letters or numbers used in enumerations as shown in the following paragraph.

> When parentheses appear with other marks of punctuation, the policy (concerning the order of the punctuation) is: **(1)** to place another punctuation mark after the close parenthesis if that mark would appear there *without the* entire parenthetic material; and **(2)** to place a punctuation mark that belongs exclusively to the parenthetic material before the close parenthesis.

Number (1) of the previous example is illustrated as follows:

> When discussing the sensuous description of the first pig killing that even Ralph seemed to enjoy **(refer to pages 165-170),** ask the students if any of them ever felt any satisfaction in squashing an ant, swatting a fly, or chasing an insect.

Number (2) is illustrated as follows:

> Please note on the last page of the document **(such a long work, too!)** that I made some small changes in the text.

Notice in the previous examples that the statement within the parentheses does not begin with a capital letter nor end with a period. However, if the statement in parentheses does not appear within a sentence, it *will* be capitalized and end with a terminal mark, as shown in the following example:

No persons are allowed in the mezzanine area until further notice. **(This is not to say that it is off limits during an emergency.)**

Brackets

Whereas parentheses indicate an additional remark (to some degree, extraneous to the body of the text), brackets, on the other hand, are inserted by the writer to clarify detail, adjust a quote, or correct a passage written by someone else.

Carlton Taft, in describing the play, stated that "His **[actor Tim Bolt's]** head was covered with a wig of human hair that hung in a fringe like an old-fashioned curtain sash."

In this quotation, the writer must use brackets to inform the reader as to identity of *his* in the original without having to quote extra material. This clarifying technique is a responsibility that the writer has to the reader whether it is an editorial comment added to a letter on *60 Minutes* or clarification of any elliptical content.

Often the writer may need to make minor changes so that the quotation will fit the syntax of the sentence.

Annandale's deteriorating condition was a "sight...not so fair / As one or two that **[the doctor had]** seen elsewhere: / An apparatus not for **[him]** to mend."

In this sentence, the words in brackets, *[the doctor had],* replaced *I have,* while *[him]* replaces *me* in the original work. Technical note: Observe the use of two previously unmentioned punctuation marks: 1) The ellipsis dots (...) indicate a series of words in the original text that have been left out; and 2) the slash or diagonal (/) lets the reader know where each line in the original poem ends. A discussion of these two marks appears in Chapter 11.

Brackets also enclose editorial corrections in quotations.

> In her review of the book she stated, "It presents an excellent view of the Battle of Hastings, which took place in 1266 **[1066].**"

> In presenting his evaluation of the new health magazine, the critic commented, "The author states that 'the more food one consumes, the greater his chance of becoming overweight'—hardy **[sic]** a new idea."

In the foregoing example, the writer of the sentence uses the Latin term *sic* in brackets to inform the reader that "that is the way it was" in the original source.

Technical note

The most effective writers try to keep the use of parentheses at a minimum by organizing their material in such a way that the use of parentheses is generally not necessary. On the other hand, the use of brackets is imperative when attempting to achieve clarity or when inserting extra information into a quotation for editorial purposes. Brackets note the insertion of the borrower's voice as distinguished from the original writer's voice. Using brackets to mark such editorial changes avoids potential claims of misquotation and protects the editor's integrity.

Practice exercise

Correct each punctuation mark that is misused and add any other punctuation marks that are needed.

1. The author mentions having read about the recent and most devastating earthquake [considering the documentation available one would seem highly unlikely] yet the book she had taken the information from still remains a mystery

2. Organize your outline to conform with the content of your research paper see the schematic design on page 44

3. The professor corrected the student's paper sarcastically commenting "Samuel Langhorne Clemens (Mark Twain) is the author of "A Keelboatmen's Story" not Ernst (*sic*) Hemingway"

4. An exclamation mark [!] not a question mark [?] should have preceded the close quotation mark

5. When I commented on how lovely her brooch was, she responded "Yes but it is terribly corrugated (corroded)"

Answers to practice exercise

1. The author mentions having read about the recent and most devastating earthquake (considering the documentation available, one would seem highly unlikely), yet the book she had taken the information from still remains a mystery.

2. Organize your outline to conform with the content of your research paper (see the schematic design on page 44).

3. The professor corrected the student's paper, sarcastically commenting, "Samuel Langhorne

Clemens [Mark Twain] is the author of "A Keelboatmen's Story," not Ernst [sic] Hemingway."

4. An exclamation mark (!), not a question mark (?), should have preceded the close quotation mark.

5. When I commented on how lovely her brooch was, she responded, "Yes, but it is terribly corrugated [corroded]."

7

The hyphen

The hyphen is technically an "en dash," whereas the dash is an "em dash." The use of the hyphen is twofold: It determines the relationship between words and between parts of words. The hyphen is an important tool that binds together series of letters into a unity of meaning. The following are various examples:

must-have issue

self-righteous

She was heavy with **antici-pation.**

She wanted to publish either **bi- or tri-weekly.**

In studying the hyphen, one must bear in mind that recommended combinations are not etched in stone. Many of the combinations, even though they may be traditional, are likely to be written differently because of the constantly changing American English. The nontraditional combinations may simply be used at the whim of a writer, or the writer may be ignorant of the traditional uses. Whatever the reason, clarity may be sacrificed, as in the case of compound adjective modifiers. Although different sources may vary, we recommend that you consult a good up-to-date, preferably unabridged, dictionary when you are uncertain as to whether a term is hyphenated. Also, following some guidelines in using the hyphen as a line-end word divider may help the reader's comprehension and speed as he or she flows along with your thoughts.

Examples of how the hyphens—or lack of hyphens—may make a difference in the meaning of a term or a sentence are illustrated in these announcements:

> The **new faculty** orientation is September 20, 1997.

> The **new-faculty** orientation is September 20, 1997.

In the first sentence, it appears that this is the first time there has been a faculty orientation—as *new* seems to modify *faculty orientation*. In the second sentence, on the other hand, it is made clear that the *new faculty* are the party to be oriented. So misunderstood is this particular use of the hyphen that it often creates ambiguous interpretations, as well as outright misinterpretations.

Don't confuse your reader. Write and punctuate so that your reader will know what you mean. Several years ago the following announcement was published:

> Now available through Continuing Education are **credit free courses.**

Those looking for an alternative college program were attracted by this bulletin but weren't quite sure what it meant. They knew it was not likely that they could get credit for free courses. When they began to ask questions, they learned that these were courses being offered without college credit. With a hyphen between the words *credit* and *free*, the minds ear would have heard the intended meaning:

Now available through Continuing Education are **credit-free** courses.

The hyphen with compound-adjective modifiers

The compound-adjective modifier is a modifier made up of two or more words used as a single idea. As is illustrated in the foregoing examples, any combination of hyphenated words acts as a single word. There are various combinations of parts of speech—such as adjective-noun, noun-adjective, participle-adverb, adverb (without -*ly*)-participle, noun combinations, etc.—all of which make compound adjectives. If these combinations appear before a noun, they are hyphenated.

Adjective-noun combination:

Parcel post packages go by **fourth-class** mail.

Verb-infinitive combination:

The cost of **made-to-order** cars is prohibitive.

Noun-participle combination:

The Pulitzer prize winner was a **world-renowned** person.

Preposition-noun combination before the composite-adjective modifier *snack bar*:

Most outdoor theaters have a **between-shows** snack bar.

Phrase-group combination:

His **matter-of-fact** attitude annoyed some, impressed others.

Noun combination:

Every fall the **Maine-New Brunswick** hillsides along the St. John River are ablaze with color.

Verb combination:

The **would-be** teachers are required to practice teach in an assigned school for a semester.

Adverb not ending in -*ly* that is hyphenated:

Dennis held the only copy of the **much-wanted** book.

Combinations that are *not* hyphenated:
The hyphen is omitted if the combination includes an adverb ending with -*ly*.

He was kept in a **heavily guarded** prison.

⇒ *Both words in combination modify* prison, *but this combination is made up of the adverb* heavily *modifying the adjective* guarded.

Also, when terms are placed after the noun—or after the verb after the noun—the hyphen is usually omitted (unless the dictionary lists the combination as hyphenated).

Most outdoor theaters have a snack bar
between shows.

His attitude was **matter-of-fact.**

⇒ *The word* matter-of-fact *is hyphenated in the dictionary.*

Because combinations with adjectives are often made up according to the needs of the writer, these forms are not generally listed in a dictionary. When these adjectives do appear in the dictionary as hyphenated compounds, they should be hyphenated in writing, even when used after the noun, because they are traditionally accepted as combinations.

Many prominent farmers have been forced into bankruptcy because they are **land-poor.**

The hyphen with various other compounds

Some combinations of words, usually nouns, are always hyphenated. Unlike compound adjectives that are often made up by the writer, hyphenated compound nouns are listed in most dictionaries.

sister-in-law

bride-to-be

secretary-treasurer

Fractions and compound numbers *twenty-one* through *ninety-nine* are always hyphenated.

He has a **two-thirds** share of the business.

The profit was **one-third** of the cost.

The skis cost him only **thirty-five** dollars.

Some words prefixed with *ex, vice, anti, pseudo, quasi, non, re,* and *self* are hyphenated before the root word. (Again, consult a dictionary when you are uncertain as to whether a word is hyphenated.)

Many electric light companies are **quasi-public.**

Ex-President Eisenhower did more to improve the highway system in the U.S. than any president before or since.

The hyphen as a line-end word divider

Perhaps the most important function of the hyphen is its use as a word divider at the end of a line when a word must be continued on to the next line, preferably at the accent point if possible.

Through the dim light of morning, the explorer forged **heroi-cally** across the virgin jungle.

Words cannot be indiscriminately divided with a hyphen. The division must occur between syllables, and thus a knowledge of proper syllabication is of special importance in using the hyphen for this purpose. Even a knowledge of syllabication is not entirely sufficient, however. There are a number of rules that must also be observed. In general, the following rules will cover most situations:

1. Words of only one syllable should never be divided nor should initials, numeric sums of money, Arabic or Roman numbers, or abbreviations.

2. Ordinarily, it is unwise to divide two-syllable words unless both syllables consist of more than two letters (Thus *also* should not be divided, but *hand-some* could easily be.)

3. Never divide a word so that a single letter stands alone at the end of a line and fewer than three letters are carried over to the next line. (For example, *a-lone* and *easi-ly*.)

4. Prefixes and suffixes allow for convenient word division, as do words containing double consonants. (For example, *dis-approve, differ-ent, sit-ting*.)

5. Compound words (such as *under-stand* or *butter-fly*) should be divided only at the natural separation of the words, and words that are already hyphenated (such as *thirty-three, hard-hearted, or eight-cylinder*) should be divided only at the hyphenated separation between the two words.

6. To achieve an appearance that provides for greater readability, words should not be divided at the ends of more than two consecutive lines, and neither should the last word of a paragraph nor the last word on a page ever be divided.

7. A proper noun should not be divided unless it is unavoidable.

8. The ending *ed* of a verb should never be carried over; it is seldom another syllable anyway. *The verb* talked, *for example, is a one-syllable word.*

9. Most readers object to a hyphenated *ing* verb ending.

10. The hyphen must come at the end of a line, not at the beginning of a line.

Your ear, your common sense, and a dictionary will perhaps be the best guides in helping you to properly divide words of two or more syllables that do not fit any of the foregoing rules. The pronunciation of a word should not be disturbed in hyphenating; therefore, accents should also be taken into consideration. In most instances, syllables of only one letter should be kept with the preceding syllable. When hyphenating the word *heroically,* for example, the *i* stays with the syllable *hero.*

Whenever possible, it is best to avoid hyphenating words, for such dividing almost invariably slows the reader's comprehension. An improperly divided word can completely break the train of thought, forcing the reader to go back and reread the divided word in order to comprehend the contextual meaning.

Hyphenated compounds

The prefix *semi* is hyphenated only with words beginning with *i* or words beginning with capital letters—for example, *semi-invalid, semi-Bohemian.* Also most compound words with prefix *self, ex,* and sometimes words with the prefixes *co, pre, pro* are hyphenated—for example, *self-employed, ex-husband, ex-President, pre-Columbian, pro-choice.* However, most words with the prefix *co, pre, pro* have dropped the hyphen—for example, *prearrange* and *cooperation.* One must check an up-to-date dictionary to know what currently is most acceptable.

The hyphen is used in a compound noun when the verb *elect* is used as a suffix. The verb *elect* then becomes part of the compound noun.

Mary is **president-elect** of her class.

The hyphen indicates an unbroken sequence.

September-June is the traditional school year.

⇒ September *to or through* June.

The 125th anniversary occurred in the school year **1964-65**.

For homework, study pages **10-22**.

A hyphen is also used to connect combinations of letters and figures, as well as from-to travel points.

An old **B-29** attempted the **New York-San Francisco** run.

In order to keep his job, hc had to join a union affiliated with the **AFL-CIO**.

Another use of the hyphen is in letter-word combinations.

X-ray, T-shirt, A-line, B-flat

Suspending hyphens

Suspending hyphens are used when the final word of the compound adjective is common to two or more of the preceding parts of the series. For example:

He ordered **five-, eight-, and ten-penny** nails.

Here, the hyphen functions as an ellipsis as one would automatically assume that *five-* and *eight-* would both be affixed to *penny*. The hyphen works in this way to achieve brevity.

The suspending hyphen is also used when referring to n part of a word such as a suffix.

All the adverbs in the sentence ended
with -**ly.**

Note: Hyphenation can be set automatically on your
computer or word processor (it is listed under "Tools" in
Word 6.0 and 7.0). However, this hyphenation tool does
have drawbacks. As you are expected to do with the spell
check, you must proofread the results of the automatic hyphenation. For example, you may get an unattractive series of hyphenations at the end of three or more consecutive lines or you may find that the tool has hyphenated a
contraction such as *do-n't.* These words should be undivided.

Practice exercise

In the following sentences hyphenate wherever
needed. Be sure your marks are intended to be hyphens
and not dashes. If the sentences require other punctuation
marks, place them where they belong. If the hyphen is
misused, correct it. You may find it necessary to write your
corrections on a separate sheet of paper.

1. Willy had a two fold purpose in taking a course
   in statistics one was to get credit toward his
   MEd the other was to earn a salary increment.

2. Years ago two thirds of furniture items were
   ready made whereas today they are assemble it
   yourself furniture even your living room
   recliner.

3. He said that it is a carefully guarded secret hardly the kind of confidence I want to betray.

4. Some speakers and writers insist on making
   nouns that end in -*ness* such as *reasonableness
   awkwardness cowardness* etc.

5. The self educated carpenter ordered 4 8 and 10 inch wide boards so that she would not have to buy a rip saw.

6. The husband protested that he had not walked out on her that her pretended vacation was a walk out on him.

7. The customer tried to tell the salesperson that bi weekly payments were not the same as semi monthly payments consequently the would be buyer walked out of the store in disgust.

Answers to practice exercise

1. Willy had a two-fold [*or* twofold] purpose in taking a course in statistics: [*or a dash*] one was to get credit toward his M.Ed., the other was to earn a salary increment.

2. Years ago, two-thirds of furniture items were ready made, whereas today they are assemble-it-yourself furniture, even your living room recliner.

3. He said that it is a carefully [*adverb modifies adjective*] guarded secret—hardly [*cannot be divided at end of line*] the kind of confidence I want to betray. *A phrase with an internal clause follows* hardly—*therefore, a dash, not a semicolon.*

4. Some speakers and writers insist on making nouns that end in -*ness* such as *reasonableness, awkwardness, cowardness,* etc.

5. The self-educated carpenter ordered 4-, 8-, and 10 inch wide boards so that she would not have to buy a rip saw.

6. The husband protested that he had not walked [*one-syllable word cannot be hyphenated*] out on her—that her pretended vacation was a walk-out on him. *The final subordinate clause could be set off by a comma instead of a dash, but the dash is stronger.*

7. The customer tried to tell the salesperson that bi-weekly payments were not the same as semi-monthly payments; consequently, the would-be buyer walked out of the store in disgust.

8

Italics and quotation marks

Quotation marks and italics are commonly—but mistakenly—used interchangeably. The more accurate uses of the two are quite specific. While it is conceivable that a particular structure could logically incorporate the use of *either* quotation marks or italics, in most writing situations there are very definite reasons why only one of these uses is correct. The practical guidelines will follow.

Although italics serve a very definite purpose in writing, they usually appeared only in published material until the advent of the IBM Selectric typewriter. In today's world with the computer, anyone who types may use italics without having to underline. However, there is no way for italics to be written effectively in longhand. In longhand and when italic print is not available, you can always resort to underscoring, which has always been employed in place of italics. Therefore, let it be understood that by italics we mean underscoring, and by underscoring we mean italics.

Quotation marks, on the other hand, set off what has actually been said or what has been previously written.

Quotation marks used in dialogue are another study that we will talk about in Chapter 10. Presently, we are concerned with titles and two other uses of italics and/or quotation marks.

Titles

In its original form, the title of one's own essay, poem, article, speech, short story, novel, etc., is *not* punctuated. However, any title referred to as a title must be punctuated, even if the author refers to his or her own title. Therefore, titles of sets of books, individual books (of any kind), pamphlets, magazines, three-act (or more) plays, movies, operas, long poems, works of art, films, radio and television shows, and newspapers are indicated by italic type (or underlined).

To Have and To Hold

Encyclopedia Britannica, Quo Vadis

The Marriage of Figaro, Evangeline, The Bangor Daily News

⇒ The *is part of the title.*

The *Record American,* The *Mona Lisa*

⇒ The *is not part of the title.*

Titles found *within* a larger volume are set off with quotation marks. For example: short stories, short poems, one-act plays, term papers, chapters from books, articles, essays, songs, and speeches are enclosed in quotation marks:

A student participates in a wide variety of game-like exercises in the **"Contemporary**

Diction" section of Ralph Lamb's *American Language Handbook.*

While applying these guidelines for punctuating titles, also learn this rule for capitalizing titles: Always capitalize the first letter of the first word, the first letter of the last word, and all the first letters of the other words in between except articles, prepositions, and conjunctions of four letters or less.

Exercise 1

Punctuate the first of the following sentences with the appropriate underscoring and/or quotation marks; then in the second sentence, with the appropriate commas and hyphens:

1. How to Say Nothing in Five Hundred Words by Paul Roberts, an essay appearing in Cox's A Reading Approach to College Writing, is aimed at prodding students into selecting more unusual subjects for their compositions.

2. Take some coughing sniffling stuffy head so you can rest medicine.

Integrating quotations into the text of a research paper

When writers borrow from one another, they use quotation marks to give credit. There is a rather set pattern as to how this is done. If the words do not run more than four or five lines, the borrower will incorporate the material into his or her own text and mark that text with quotation marks. For example:

1. In the thesis statement of her term paper the author comments that **"in order to**

> **use the comma…according to the**
> **structural patterns recognized by editors**
> **and publishers, the writer must have a**
> **knowledge of the fundamentals of**
> **grammar" (Dyer 11).**

Observe in this example that the first word of the quoted material is not capitalized, because the quotation breaks into the middle of the original statement. Also note that ellipsis dots are used to indicate that some words that appear in the original have been left out.

In preparing a research paper, a writer may find a unique idea in the source materials that communicates exactly what he or she needs to relate to the reader. The researcher may then lift the words—word-for-word—from that source and weave them into his or her own writing. When quoting, always copy the exact words of the author. Then make sure the borrowed passage flows smoothly in and out of its new context.

> 2. Willis states that **"putting bibliographic**
> **information on a 3- by 5-inch card is**
> **important" (395),** because the researcher
> in this way **"can check out a book or**
> **periodical without returning to the card**
> **catalog or periodical index…" (Willis**
> **396).**

The foregoing information illustrates the 1995 Modern Language Association (MLA) style guidelines—the "new system of documentation [in which] brief parenthetical citations in the text refer to a bibliography at the end of the research paper, thus eliminating the need for all but explanatory footnotes…" (Gibaldi, "Preface for the Instructor").

When the quoted material exceeds four or five lines, type the quoted lines in indented block form five spaces (or a quarter of an inch) from the left margin, with a double space before the quotation. Because of the indented block form, no quotation marks are necessary unless they already appear in some part of the original source.

3. It is imperative that ideas gathered for a research paper eventually be put in a well-organized pattern. Therefore, in order to achieve this goal, a tentative or working outline has a threefold purpose in that

> **it forces you [the researcher]: (a) to take stock of the information you already have, (b) to limit your subject by thinking seriously about what information you expect to find, and (c) to provide an efficient means for you to record your reading on note cards [or on your Worksheet pages] under the proper headings. (Hook 46)**

Note: (1) The word *that,* preceding a quotation, needs no punctuation before or after it as you may note in examples 1 and 2. (2) The brackets in example 3 indicate the words of the researcher, not the words of Hook, who is the author of the quotation. (3) After a long, indented quotation, as in example 3, the period goes before the parenthetical reference. In all other documentation the period is after the close parenthesis of the parenthetical reference.

Other uses of italics

Names of ships, trains, aircraft, spacecraft, and other objects with names should be italicized or underscored.

The Ocean Monarch

The Aroostook Flyer

The Winnie May

The Challenger

Foreign words or expressions that are not yet regarded as English are italicized. A good college desk dictionary ordinarily uses some device to indicate when a foreign term has been anglicized.

> When the European asked for a ***pamplemousse,*** the waitress handed him the dessert menu.

> The lumberjacks were getting tired of beans and sauerkraut.

⇒ *The German word* sauerkraut, *meaning "sour cabbage," has been anglicized; the French word for grapefruit*—pamplemousse—*has not.*

Exercise 2

Punctuate the following with the proper underscoring and/or quotation marks:

1. The early English comedy Ralph Roister Doister is an example of jeu d'esprit.

Words referred to

Words, letters, and numbers that are taken out of context or that are being referred to as words, letters, and numbers should be italicized. (The definition of a word, however, may be put in quotation marks, as in the following second and third examples.)

> The word *these* appeared six times in one of his sentences.

> The German word ***sauerkraut,*** meaning **"sour cabbage,"** has been anglicized.

⇒ *Now* sauerkraut *is italicized because it's being referred to as a word.*

> The preposition *via* means **"by way of."**

> She wrote ***corrugated*** when she meant ***corroded.***

> Her *t*'s look like *x*'s.

> She uses ***but*'**s when she could use ***however*'s** in her sentences.

Instead of using italics, you can underline the two preceding examples as follows:

> Her **t**'s look like **x**'s.

> She uses **but**'s when she could use **however**'s in her sentences.

If you look closely at the last four examples, the word is either in italics or underlined, but the *s* that makes them plural is not in italics nor underlined (see pages 132-133 about the plurals that are formed with an apostrophe, but don't misunderstand this rule—unless they are letters, signs, figures, symbols, or words referred to as *words*, nouns do *not* form their plurals with an apostrophe *s*).

Emphasized words

Finally, underscoring (or italics) can be used to give emphasis, but overloading a paper with underscoring—as we have seen similarly with the exclamation point—can weaken its effectiveness. A writer should reserve underscoring so that it will appear only when there is a definite purpose for using it.

> Contrary to popular belief, Herman **was** present at the meeting last Tuesday.

The underscoring (or italics) is necessary in the preceding sentence as it emphasizes the specific change in the occurring idea. Read aloud the following sentences to observe the difference:

> Herman was present.

> Herman **was** present this time.

Quotation marks may also be used to enclose a word emphasized—a word that may not be the writer's choice:

> Betsy grimaced when her boss commented on the poor performance of the **"office grunts."**

Exercise 3

Put to work what you have learned about the punctuation marks up to and including the uses of quotation marks. If you are rewriting these sentences on a computer, use italics when they are called for. However, if you do not have access to a computer and you are handwriting your answers, then be sure to underline all words that would normally be italicized in print. (One *cannot* draw italics.)

1. Traditionally synecdoche has meant the use of the part for the whole and metonymy has meant the substitution of one thing for another thing with which it is closely related today the terms seem to have become less specific because both terms are appearing as one metonymy.

2. Examples of metonymy are the crown for king and light for fire

3. In the poem Spring by William Shakespeare the term married ear means a married man.

4. Our article A Tree Like Me was published in the Fall 1976 issue of Exercise Exchange.

5. My memoirs Memories Are Made of This... are written in an anecdotal fashion to avoid a strict chronological approach

6. The title of my memoirs is taken from words sung by Dean Martin and the title of my poem ...easing the Spring is taken out of context from a line in Naming of Parts a poem by Henry Reed.

Answers to the exercises

Exercise 1

1. "How to Say Nothing in Five Hundred Words" by Paul Roberts, an essay appearing in Cox's **A Reading Approach to College Writing**, is aimed at prodding students into selecting more unusual subjects for their compositions.

2. Take some coughing, sniffling, stuffy-head, so-you-can-rest medicine.

Exercise 2

1. The early English comedy **Ralph Roister Doister** is an example of **jeu d'esprit**.

Exercise 3

1. Traditionally **synecdoche** has meant "the use of the part for the whole" and **metonymy** has meant "the substitution of one thing for another thing with which it is closely related"; today the terms seem to have become less specific because both terms are appearing as one: [*or dash*] **metonymy**. *(In this exercise we are assuming the corrections are being written out in long hand; thus the use of underlining titles in place of italics.)*

2. Examples of metonymy are "the crown" for king and "light" for fire.

3. In the poem "Spring" by William Shakespeare, the term **married ear** means "a married man."

4. Our article "A Tree Like Me" was published in the Fall 1976 issue of **Exercise Exchange**. *(Usually seasons are not capitalized—see Rule 1 in Chapter 13. Because* Fall *is the issue date of* Exercise Exchange, *it may be capitalized.)*

5. My memoirs, **Memories Are Made of This...**, are written in an anecdotal fashion to avoid a strict chronological approach.

6. The title of my memoirs is taken from words sung by Dean Martin, and the title of my poem "...easing the Spring" is taken out of context from a line in "Naming of Parts," a poem by Henry Reed. *(Notice the noncapitalization of the poem "...easing the Spring"—a freedom a writer feels comfortable with once he or she has a good grasp on the punctuation rules.)*

9

The apostrophe

The apostrophe has three main uses: to show possession; to indicate a contraction; and to pluralize letters, figures, signs, symbols, and words taken out of context or referred to *as* words.

In this section a few exercises have been inserted to enable you to understand more fully the concepts in the uses of the apostrophe. Be aware that the rules governing the use of the apostrophe are very specific in the same way that the English language is particular in the way it pluralizes, makes possessive, and contracts words.

Possessives

Whether a noun is singular or plural, making the word possessive is a simple matter. A noun that does not end in *s* is made possessive by adding an apostrophe and *s* ('*s*). A noun that *does* end in *s* is made possessive by adding an apostrophe after the *s* (*s*'). *Remember a noun's singular or plural form has nothing to do with making it possessive.*

Give the **boy's** ball back to him.

The cheek in the **bass'** head is a delicacy.

⇒ *An earlier form did add apostrophe s ('s) to a singular word ending in s (St. James's, bass's).*

Exercise 1

In the following phrases, make each of the nouns possessive by adding *'s* or just an apostrophe to the noun already ending in an *s:*

1. the child toy
2. two weeks pay
3. a week pay
4. James situation
5. men clothing

6. ladies shop
7. the children toys
8. girls dorm
9. women apparel
10. boss job

In addition to nouns that form their possessives in the standard manner, some of the indefinite pronouns having to do with people, such as *anyone, no one, someone,* and *everybody,* also form their possessives by adding *'s.* Note that this rule applies to only the indefinite pronouns and none of the other pronouns (see the Glossary for a complete list).

It was **anybody's** guess as to who would win first prize.

Someone's glove was left on the chair.

Exercise 2

Apply the preceding rule to the following sentences:

1. This is somebody else book.
2. That is anybody guess.

Apostrophes are *not* used in the possessive forms of personal pronouns, which are in themselves possessive:

my, his, hers, its, ours, theirs, yours

Each of the indefinite pronouns—*each, everyone,* and *anyone*—is singular.

Each of you is responsible for your own coat.

Everyone is wearing a hat.

⇒ *The word* is *is correct because of the subjects* each *and* everyone.

Anyone's memory, at any age, **is** likely to play tricks on him or her.

A compound noun or a compound indefinite pronoun is made possessive by adding an apostrophe and an *s* to the last word.

My **daughter-in-law's** family lives next door.

This is my **parents-in-law's** house.

⇒ *Observe in this example that the most important word,* parents, *is pluralized, but the last word in the compound,* law, *has the 's for the possessive form.*

Exercise 3

Make two words in the following sentence possessive:

1. Each one room will be designed according to the individual taste.

If the writer wishes to indicate joint ownership, only the last-named member is made possessive, while if the writer wishes to indicate separate ownership, each of the names will be made possessive.

> We ate at **Joe and Mary's** Restaurant.

> The teachers were expected to interview **James, Timothy, and Michael's** parents.

> ⇒ *All three boys have the same parents.*

> The teachers were expected to interview **James', Timothy's, and Michael's** parents.

> ⇒ *Each boy has different parents.*

The apostrophe is often omitted from the name of an organization:

> Westfield State College was formerly **Westfield State Teachers College.**

Contractions and omissions

An apostrophe may indicate that some letters (or numbers) have been left out. These forms are known as contractions. Such omissions are not often used in formal letters or literature.

> **Don't** let go of the rope.
> (**Do not** let go of the rope.)

He **should've** been here on time. **It's** already
8 a.m.
(He **should have** been here on time. **It is**
already 8 a.m.)

If we leave now, **we'll** get to meet with the
class of **'82**.
(If we leave now, **wc will** get to meet with the
class of **1982**.)

The apostrophe is often used to mark the omission of
the first two digits of a year—for example, the '60s and
'70s generation. With these uses of the apostrophe, one
becomes more convinced that the plurals of years, temperature degrees, numbers, etc., probably should add just *s*
instead of *'s*. (Note that to place the closing apostrophe before the abbreviated date on a computer, one has to trick
the computer by typing the apostrophe separately from the
number and then deleting the space between the number
and the closing single quotation mark; otherwise, as you
will experience, the result will be *'s*.)

Be alert to the distinction of possessives and contractions
such as *its* and *it's; whose* and *who's; there, they're,* and
their. The following exercises will test these distinctions.

Exercise 4

Place apostrophes where they belong in the following
sentences when the apostrophe is necessary.

1. Its about time you got home!

2. Do you like its new name?

3. Whos at the door?

4. Whose book is this?

5. Theyre off.

6. Theres the winner.

There are some contractions that don't quite follow the rules, such as *shan't, won't* and *ain't,* because there are no clear-cut combinations of words to justify the contraction. For example, the contraction of *it's* is *it is; don't, do not; they're, they are;* etc. However, does *shan't* mean *shall not* and *won't* mean *would not?* As for "Ain't I", does it mean, "Am I not?" Does "He ain't here" mean "He isn't here"? These last few contractions appear to have meaning, even though they don't follow the rules. Maybe this is the reason for classifying them as colloquial or, more recently, nonstandard.

Plurals

Traditionally, an apostrophe and an *s* are used to form the plurals of letters, figures, signs, symbols, and words taken out of context or referred to as words. However, more writers have chosen to just add *s.* (Remember, though, that letters, numbers, and words referred to as letters, numbers, and words are either underlined or in italics, but the *'s* or just the *s*—whichever you prefer—is not in italics.)

> To have all **B's** and **A's** on a college transcript is exceptional.

or

> To have all **Bs** and **As**...

⇒ *Grades do not need to be in italics.*

The space age started in the early **1960's.**

or

The space age started in the early **1960s**.

⇒ *Years do not need to be in italics.*

You have five ***and'* s** in that sentence.

or

You have five ***ands*** in that sentence.

⇒ *Words in italics. (See pages 122-123.)*

The ***6'*** s in the box should have a line under them, so you won't mix them up with ***9'*** s.

In your account book make sure you use **+'s** and **-'s**.

⇒ *It is difficult to make the plural symbols the way you intend them without the apostrophe.*

Remember that to form the plural of a nonpossessive noun, just add *s*—never *'s* or *s'*. This rule also applies to a third-person, singular verb in the present tense.

The **girls** enjoyed their summer counseling **jobs**.

⇒ *The words* girls *and* jobs *are plural nouns, no apostrophes!*

Finally, if you are considering having a sign in front of your house identifying the name of your family, make the name plural with *no apostrophes.*

Alward becomes **The Alwards**.

Rogers becomes **The Rogerses**.

Fleury becomes **The Fleurys**.

Exercise 5

1. All CDs are discounted twenty five percent at Bernies Appliance Store during their big Presidents Day sale.

2. The temperature has risen into the 50s on this date February 18 1997.

3. Phil and Dale religious views conflict in every discussion we have. (*Make one name or both names possessive.*)

4. The war years of the 40s were too horrendous for that generation of the Soucy, the Williams, and the Tauro to talk about. (*Punctuate 40s and make the family names plural.*)

Answers to the exercises

Exercise 1

1. the child's toy
2. two weeks' pay
3. a week's pay
4. James' situation
5. men's clothing
6. ladies' shop
7. the children's toys
8. girls' dorm
9. women's apparel
10. boss' job

Exercise 2

1. This is somebody else's book.
2. That is anybody's guess.

Exercise 3

1. Each one's room will be designed according to the individual's taste.

Exercise 4

1. It's about time you got home!
2. Do you like its new name? *(Correct as is.)*
3. Who's at the door?
4. Whose book is this? *(Correct as is.)*
5. They're off.
6. There's the winner.

Exercise 5

1. All CD's are discounted twenty-five percent at Bernie's Appliance Store during their big Presidents' Day sale.
2. The temperature has risen into the 50s on this date: *[Or a dash instead of a colon]* February 18, 1997. *(Either* 50's *or* 50s.*)*
3. Phil's and Dale's religious views conflict in every discussion we have.
4. The war years of the '40s were too horrendous for that generation of the Soucys, the Williamses, and the Tauros to talk about.

10

Quotation marks in dialogue

Quotation marks set off what has actually been said or what has previously been written. Opening quotation marks are placed before the reproduced material and closing quotation marks, at the end of the reproduced material.

In England single quotation marks are used to set off dialogue—a usage that is becoming increasingly popular in the United States, especially in journalistic writing. Nevertheless, double quotation marks are traditionally used in this country and are, consequently, recommended. In either country, double and single quotation marks are alternated when discerning quotations within quotations.

Quotation marks, like parentheses and brackets, are used with other punctuation marks. The order in which they appear thus becomes a complicated issue. The American tradition is to put commas and periods inside the closing quotation marks, the English is to put them outside. Semicolons, dashes and colons immediately follow the closing quotation marks.

Her poem about the ant is entitled "Summer Visitor."

At one time the automobile had what was called a "running board," but that part of the car has long since disappeared.

His own way of life proved that He meant all mankind when He said, "Whatever you would have men do to you do you also to them"; but what a shame that we so often break this Golden Rule.

Quoted dialogue

What one has said or is saying appears in narrative writing as dialogue, because the writer attempts to discern what he or she has written from what he or she is quoting (or pretends to quote). This quoted dialogue is distinguished by quotation marks. (Please note that dialogue in story-telling requires a new paragraph for each change of speakers.)

"Hello," she greeted. "Are you lost?"

"No, I wasn't until I met you," he replied as he gazed into her dark blue eyes.

"What is wrong with me!" she exploded, misinterpreting his remark.

Quotation marks in relation to other punctuation marks

Regarding the manner in which it appears with other punctuation marks, quoted material probably has more mechanical details to observe than any other written material. The examples that follow will attempt to display these details.

When the speaker is identified at the opening of the sentence, a comma is used before the quotation and the quoted statement begins with a capital letter.

Mary said, "I have no lamb today."

Jim asked, "Why not?"

When a quotation is completed before the speaker is identified, a comma appears after the quoted statement and before the closing quotation mark. The speaker or "tag" (see glossary) then completes the sentence.

"He plays to win," **she jollied.**

If the quoted material is a question or an exclamation, the question mark or exclamation mark precedes the closing quotation mark. This is true no matter where the quotation appears in the sentence.

"Who is at the door?" she screamed.

The man exclaimed, "What a dull show!"

If the sentence containing the quotation is itself a question or exclamation, then the end mark will follow the closing quotation mark.

Who said, "All the world is a stage, and we are its actors"?

⇒ *Be sure to observe that there is no period preceding the closing quotation mark.*

Furthermore, a quoted question appearing within a sentence that is itself a question requires only one end mark. In the case of the previous example, the question mark would precede the closing quotation mark.

Who asked, "Where are you?"

Whether the quotation is a question within a statement or vice versa or a question within another question, *only one terminal mark should be used to end the sentence.* Illustrations of this rule appear throughout this chapter.

The first example sentence that follows is transformed into a quotation in the second example by inserting the identification of the speaker. To do this, the writer breaks the statement into two understandable pieces and places them on either side of the inserted explanatory interruption or tag. Opening and closing quotation marks frame each fragment of the original statement. Note the manner in which commas are used to set off the interruption:

The only important thing in life is to live each day as though it were your last.

"The only important thing in life," **he philosophized,** "is to live each day as though it were your last."

Because the quoted material is one complete independent element (the comma after *philosophized* conveys this), the resumed quotation does not begin with a capital letter.

When a quotation is interrupted by a tag between two complete ideas (independent clauses), the mark of punctuation that would normally appear after the first independent clause will appear after the tag.

"Everyone's life is made better for having known him," **Peg remarked; "his** humor delights each individual in a crowd."

"The house will be completed by September," **the contractor estimated.** "The roofing and siding are being put on now."

When a quotation is interrupted by an explanation of the situation (rather than a tag), a dash precedes the closing quotation mark, and the statement following the interruption begins with a capital.

"He is playing near the riverbank where we used to—" **She** stopped suddenly as she realized that the child had disappeared.

⇒ *Notice that in this structuring the dash is inside the closing quotation mark.*

It appears that question marks and exclamation marks are typically the gremlins that throw off one's understanding of other punctuation used in conjunction with quotation marks. As these two end marks are so flexible in their placement, it seems contradictory that commas and periods are always placed inside and semicolons and colons outside the closing quotation mark. Alas, these are the traditions we have to work with. Nonetheless, we must remember that these four marks (comma, period, colon, semicolon) are quite fixed in their placement, whereas the exclamation mark, the question mark, and sometimes the dash, as well, are not.

"Will you be able to keep our dinner engagement?" the young man pleaded.

"What a slob!" the girls cried when they saw
his long greasy hair.

Did you notice the tone of sarcasm in her
voice when Marie remarked, "You will love
Mr. Copeland"?

What a shock it was to hear him say,
"You're fired"!

"Do you think that—" he started to say to
Beth as Molly zoomed into the room.

The guest speaker—he recited "The Cataract
of Lodore"—overwhelmed the listeners with
his dramatic oratory.

A good rule of thumb on the placement of punctuation
marks with quotation marks can be summed up like this:
Whereas a comma and a period fall inside the closing
quotation mark (," and ."), a colon, a semicolon, and usually a dash fall beyond the closing quotation mark ("; and
": and "—). The bibliographic reference following a direct
quotation creates an exception to the rule of putting the
period and the comma inside the closing of a quotation.

Willis states that "putting bibliographic
information on a 3- by 5-inch card is
important" **(395),** because the researcher in
this way "can check out a book or periodical
without returning to the card catalog or
periodical index..." **(Willis 396).**

Quotations within quotations

Quotations within quotations, as already mentioned,
are punctuated by using double and single quotation

marks alternately. The writer begins with double quotation marks and then uses single marks for internal quotations. If the writer should need a third quotation, which would appear within the single quotation marks, he or she would revert to the use of the double quotation marks.

> Jill pondered in reply, "I don't want any
> candy because my mother just said to me,
> 'Jill, do you know what I mean by "no
> lunching before meals"'?' "

It is best to revise such combinations if possible and avoid alternating quotation marks.

Indirect discourse

Indirect discourse is information that has been said or thought but does not appear in the same manner in which it originally did. Paraphrasing, like indirect discourse, is the restating of the sense of the passage borrowed. Do not use quotation marks to set off indirect discourse. In the following, the first is an indirect quotation while the second is direct.

> The dealer said that I ought to buy a
> Rambler for a second car.

> The dealer said, "You ought to buy a
> Rambler for a second car."

Notice the change of pronouns from the *I* for indirect address to the *you* for direct address.

Sometimes the writer must decide whether a statement is to be direct or indirect.

Who said a double negative makes a positive?

Who said, "A double negative makes a positive"?

In the first sentence of the previous examples, the word *that* is understood as belonging after *said*, making this an indirect quotation.

Quoted fragments

When a quotation is only a fragment of the borrowed wording or a definition, the first word is not capitalized unless it is a proper name or the first word in a sentence. The first word and the words that follow are also woven into the sentence so that they need no commas before or after them. Remember this form for well-integrated source quotations in research-paper writing.

The English instructor called the theme **"a reflection of immaturity."**

The preposition *via* means **"by way of."**

Like the comma, quotation marks are an exacting and complicated mark of punctuation to apply correctly. Close attention to the rules for correct usage, however, will preclude any danger of using these marks inaccurately. To review more about this complicated mark and its counterpart, italics, refer to Chapter 8.

Practice exercise

1. The old dog barks backward without getting up Frost writes in his poem The Span of Life I can remember when he was a pup.

2. Dora you have too many ands buts and sos in your essay the English teacher explained Why don't you try using some conjunctive adverbs such as however, moreover consequently for variety.

3. Edgar Dad emphasized as I left the house I want you in this house by 10 pm.

4. The Dean wanted to know whether I would be using Catcher in the Rye Death of a Salesman or Lord of the Flies in English Composition II.

5. Most of the snow the instructor commented has melted on the eastern ski trail. Don't you think it would be safer to use the trail on the other side of Mt. Snow instead.

Answers to practice exercise

1. "The old dog barks backward without getting up," Frost writes in his poem "The Span of Life." "I can remember when he was a pup."

2. "Dora, you have too many <u>and</u>'s, <u>but</u>'s, and <u>so</u>'s in your essay," the English teacher explained. "Why don't you try using some conjunctive adverbs such as <u>however</u>, <u>moreover</u>, and <u>consequently</u> for variety." (*Remember that in print, italics would be used for underlining.*)

3. "Edgar," Dad emphasized as I left the house, "I want you in this house by 10 p.m."

4. The Dean wanted to know whether I would be using <u>Catcher in the Rye</u>, <u>Death of a Salesman</u>, or <u>Lord of the Flies</u> in English Composition II.

5. "Most of the snow," the instructor commented, "has melted on the eastern ski trail. Don't you think it would be safer to use the trail on the other side of Mt. Snow instead?"

11

Miscellaneous punctuation marks and characters

Beyond the marks of punctuation already discussed, there are other marks that are minor or, in some cases, obsolete. Some of these may not be considered punctuation at all but merely characters that have appeared or may appear in some writing.

Among these miscellaneous marks are the following:

1. The asterisk (*) is a reference mark indicating that there is additional information in the footnote or in some other part of the book that relates to the text directly preceding the asterisk.

2. Similar in use to the asterisk, the dagger (†) and double dagger (‡) are seldom used and have largely been replaced by the consecutive raised numbering of additional notes.

3. A diagonal (/)—sometimes called a slash, bar, or virgule—is generally used to convey the expression *and/or* and to separate initials of the dictator and the transcriber of a letter, popularly known as a stenographic reference (e.g., ECA/da). The diagonal may also be used to separate lines of poetry quoted within the context of a report or research paper.

   Many feel that the following lines from Elizabeth Barrett Browning's 43rd sonnet are their favorite: "How do I love thee? Let me count the ways. / I love thee to the depth and breadth and height / My soul can reach...."

   In statistical information, but not in formal writing, one may use diagonals to represent the day (6/4/96) or to note fractions (such as 3/10).

4. The brace ({ }) has been used to connect a number of words with one common term, a use that is generally avoided.

   spruce
   evergreens {
   cedar

5. Ditto marks are often considered a time-saving device, but they are not recommended for formal writing. They may be used in note-taking and in tabulating to list words or phrases where some amount of repetition occurs.

6. Ellipsis dots—three of them—indicate the omission of unnecessary or irrelevant material within a quotation, or sometimes at the beginning of a sentence. Four ellipsis dots indicate that one or more sentences have been omitted or that the words omitted came at the end of a sentence.

The research paper concluded that "few American public figures...have written so many books, delivered so many letters,...advocated so many causes.... They also got mixed up in many scandals, were spied on, tricked and left holding the bag...." so wrote Robert Cantwell about Upton Sinclair in the February 1937 issue of *The New Republic*.

12

Arbitrary uses
of punctuation

Several times throughout this book we have implied that to some degree punctuation may be arbitrary. On a plaque that appears in one of America's scenic natural-wonder areas, there is the following inscription that—as you can readily see—far exceeds the bounds of arbitrary punctuation:

> The mountain before you is part of the
> Appalachian chain—they are some of the
> oldest mountains in the world—at one time;
> in elevation, they were higher than the
> Rockies—and in the Rockies today, there are
> over 30 peaks higher than 14,000 feet above
> sea level.

When punctuation can be arbitrary, its use depends upon the discretion of the writer; and thus there is no comprehensive way to explain each and every use in this category. Various arbitrary uses of punctuation marks have already been discussed. Other arbitrary uses will be discussed and illustrated in this chapter.

Although a person should have a basic knowledge of punctuation before attempting any type of writing, he or she need not be an expert in the field in order to punctuate effectively in arbitrary situations. Any use of punctuation that can be logically explained and leaves the sentence structurally intact should be acceptable. The thing to remember, however, is that while one usage may be entirely correct, another usage may have more effect on the reader.

Earlier in this book, it was recommended that when one or both independent clauses in a compound sentence are internally punctuated, the comma before the coordinate conjunction is strengthened to a semicolon (see Chapter 3). Yet the following sentence appears stilted with a semicolon at this point and would probably look and read a lot better with a comma where the semicolon appears.

> If we can be of any further assistance, please
> let us know; and we will have our company
> representative call at your store.

Conversely, if the following sentence does not have a semicolon before the *and*, it may be misread:

> Pleasing our guests is the most important
> function of a Vacation Inn; and you, one of
> our most important people, can help us
> greatly by answering these questions.

Normally, a prepositional phrase embedded in a sentence is not set off by commas. There are occasions, however, when the writer may have a long phrasal element that has interrupted the thought that began the sentence.

> Through the centuries, **from the time of the
> Greek invention of punctuation,** there

appears to have been no orderly system of punctuation.

⇒ *There must be a comma after the word* punctuation, *but there also has to be a comma after* centuries *in order to continue the thought that "through
the centuries...there appears...."*

A prepositional phrase embedded within a sentence
may be set off by commas when it is introduced by *of* and
indicates connection.

Dr. Douglas Murray, **of Omaha, Nebraska,**
will be our guest speaker at the
homecoming.

Depending upon the purpose the writer may have in
mind, a simple introductory prepositional phrase, which is
usually not set off, may be intended to convey emphasis.

With little effort, he scaled the top of the
huge pile of pulp wood.

The one-syllable conjunctive adverbs *then, thus, hence;*
the two-syllable conjunctive adverb *also;* and the adverb
too are not usually set off by commas. Yet the writer may
on occasion want to put emphasis on one of these words.

He **then** went to the store.

This, **then,** is the way I must plan to attack
the problem.

Subordinate adverbial clauses that follow independent
clauses normally are not set off by a comma, but there are

instances when these clauses may seem more effective or more emphatic when set off.

1. When the dependent clause of reason is introduced by *as, since, inasmuch as,* or *because.*

   He should be on time this morning, **because** he knows how much work we have to do.

2. When a clause of condition follows the independent clause and is introduced by *provided, provided that,* or *except that.*

   We will have picked all the potatoes by tomorrow afternoon, **provided it doesn't snow tonight.**

3. When a clause of concession follows the independent clause.

   We voted for Dale, **although we knew the majority favored Hayley for president.**

When an adverbial clause falls within a restrictive clause, writers should omit the comma before the adverbial clause; but in most instances, they should place one after it.

   The thing to remember is that **while the launching may be delayed,** the safety of the men in the capsule has been assured.

   ⇒ *The reader could be misled into assuming the adverb clause to be nonessential; therefore, no comma is placed between that and while.*

Another variation of this is found in this example:

   When an adverbial clause falls within a restrictive clause, writers should omit the comma before the adverbial clause; **but in most instances,** they should place one after it.

⇒ *It is better to have no comma between* but *and* in.

To avoid awkwardness in the preceding example, it would be even better to reconstruct the second clause.

When an adverbial clause falls within a restrictive clause, writers should omit the comma before the adverbial clause; but they should, **in most instances,** place one after it.

If a sentence intends to introduce or amplify a thought or series, a colon may be used instead of a period. In this case the statement following the colon may begin with a capital letter.

You have one possibility of obtaining that 2.0 average: Earn a B in this course.

Several things must be done to splice a film properly: The film must be cut so that the ends will overlap. The emulsion on one of the overlapping ends must be thoroughly scraped off. A film cement or solvent is applied to one of these ends. Finally, pressure is immediately applied for about 30 seconds.

Some arbitrary uses are so much a part of the individual's style of writing that the writer is the only one who can determine the punctuation, as is illustrated in the following examples.

Red and white blocks, green and yellow
blocks, amused the baby.

George Gibbs in the play *Our Town* seemed,
at one time in his life, to be asking, "Why
shouldn't Mother cook, sew, wash, iron—
and chop wood?"

⇒ *The dash, rather than a comma, implies that
George's mother, according to George, should be
able to do all her regular work as well as "chop
wood."*

Clarity—above all else—must be considered in effective writing. The writer should therefore keep in mind that
any arbitrary uses of punctuation should be carefully
geared with this end in view: to assure maximum comprehension and readability. All punctuation, both standard and
arbitrary, should be applied so as to present the writer's
thoughts in as clear and precise a manner as possible.

13

Capitalization

The following tells and shows you when and when not to capitalize:

1. Capitalize a person's name and a person's title when it precedes the name; days of the week, months of the year (not the seasons of the year), and special days; organizations and abbreviations of organizations; races and languages; historical periods, events, and documents; words pertaining to the Deity (in all religions); and personifications of objects and abstract concepts.

2. Capitalize the first word of a statement and a quoted sentence within a statement, but not a quoted phrase blended into a sentence.

3. Capitalize high school, college, street, park, lake, river, country, company, society, institution, etc., when used as an essential part of a proper name. However, when used alone as a substitute for a proper name, each one appears in the lowercase form as shown here.

4. Capitalize a noun designating a family relationship when substituted for a proper name.

   Is **Dad** home?

   My dad is home.

5. Capitalize geographical locations, but not mere points on a compass.

   The South is warm.

   He went **west**.

   ⇒ *He traveled in a westerly direction.*

6. In a title, capitalize the first letter of all the words except prepositions, articles, and conjunctions of four letters or less. Always capitalize the first letter of the first and last words of the title.

   Up the Down Staircase

   ⇒ Down *in this title is an adjective.*

   Now, note *down* as a preposition:

   Alice Falls down the Rabbit Hole

7. In an outline, capitalize only the first word of each item, always remembering any proper noun that appears is also capitalized. However, the table of contents, used in an extended work such as a book, follows Rule 6 above, because each item is a title in the book.

8. Capitalize the pronoun *I*.

9. Capitalize the names of subjects studied when they are specific titles or when they are derived from a proper name.

   I am taking **Psychology II, math, geology, and English.**

   ⇒ *Whether they are subjects or specific titles, names of languages are always capitalized.*

10. Capitalize acronyms.

    AT&T made a collect call to the **AFL/CIO** in Washington, D.C.

    Exceptions are items that have been incorporated into the language; for example, laser stands for "light amplification by stimulated emission of radiation." A good up-to-date desk dictionary will tell you which acronyms have become common words.

11. Capitalize the *Dear* in the salutation of a letter and the first word in the complimentary close.

    Sincerely yours,

14

Abbreviations and numbers

Abbreviations

Disregarding the fact that notes written for personal use are often abbreviated, in all other writing you should avoid abbreviations. Obviously, the exceptions tend to be somewhat arbitrary; nonetheless, there are conventional uses that are appropriate:

1. Initials with a person's name.

   Robert **C.** Brown

   ⇒ *This helps to distinguish him from the other Robert Browns.*

   W.C. Fields

   ⇒ *Some people, particularly those who have earned distinction, prefer initials with last names.*

2. Titles before proper names.

Mr. James Appleton

Rev. Victoria Safford

Dr. Linda Levine

Prof. Wallace Goldstein

3. Formal titles following names.

Stephen Dorey, **LL.D.**

Catherine Dower, **Ph.D.**

George R. Alward, **Jr.**

4. Some abbreviations that have to do with date and time.

Sophocles died in **498 A.D.**

⇒ *No space after the dots.*

We were to leave on the fishing trip to Cape Cod at **5 a.m.**

⇒ *Again no space after the dots.*

5. Abbreviations for names of business organizations used in place of writing out the full name of the company.

C.B.C. (for Campus Business Computers)

However, most companies, radio and television stations, and government agencies now prefer to use the abbreviations without the dots.

The following abbreviations have become readable without the full-stop period:

AT&T, TRW, NBC, WABC, CIA, FBI

There is also the tendency to omit the full-stop periods in abbreviations like **US, USA, USSR, WC** Fields. Similarly, many company abbreviations have become acronyms—that is, words formed from the initial letters.

NATO *(for* North Atlantic Treaty Organization*)*

PAC *(for* Political Action Committee*)*

WAC *(for* Women's Army Corps.*)*

Eventually, some acronyms become common names, such as *radar* for "radio detecting *and* ranging."

6. Reference notes in research papers, dissertations, and other documented writings that refer to page numbers: *p.* for one page and *pp.* for two or more pages.

7. Ampersands (&), unless they are a part of a company name, are unacceptable in normal writing (see *ampersand* in glossary). The lower case ampersand (∂) , unless used in one's personal note taking, is also unacceptable in all writing to be read by your reader.

Several years ago the United States Postal Service changed the abbreviations of states and territories of the United States and Canada to code letters (see the accompanying chart on page 161). Most recently, the United States Postal Service has recommended that the code letters not be separated from the city with a comma.

Westhampton MA 01027-9500

U.S. Postal Two-letter code for States, Territories, and Provinces

U.S. state/territory	Abbreviation	U.S. state/territory	Abbreviation
Alabama	AL	Missouri	MO
Alaska	AK	Montana	MT
Arizona	AZ	Nebraska	NE
Arkansas	AR	Nevada	NV
American Samoa	AS	New Hampshire	NH
California	CA	New Jersey	NJ
Canal Zone	CZ	New Mexico	NM
Colorado	CO	New York	NY
Connecticut	CT	North Carolina	NC
Delaware	DE	North Dakota	ND
District of	DC	Ohio	OH
Columbia		Oklahoma	OK
Florida	FL	Oregon	OR
Georgia	GA	Pennsylvania	PA
Guam	GU	Puerto Rico	PR
Hawaii	HI	Rhode Island	RI
Idaho	ID	South Carolina	SC
Illinois	IL	South Dakota	SD
Indiana	IN	Tennessee	TN
Iowa	IA	Trust Territories	TT
Kansas	KS	Texas	TX
Kentucky	KY	Utah	UT
Lousiana	LA	Vermont	VT
Maine	ME	Virginia	VA
Maryland	MD	Virgin Islands	VI
Massachusetts	MA	Washington	WA
Michigan	MI	West Virginia	WV
Minnesota	MN	Wisconsin	WI
Mississippi	MS	Wyoming	WY

Canadian province	Abbreviation	Canadian province	Abbreviation
Alberta	AB	Nova Scotia	NS
British Columbia	BC	Ontario	ON
Labrador	LB	Prince Edward	PE
Manitoba	MB	Island	
New Brunswick	NB	Quebec	PQ
Newfoundland	NF	Saskatchewan	SK
Northwest	NT	Yukon Territory	YT
Territories			

Note: Abbreviations are normally two or more letters followed by a period (Ma. or Mass.). Since the postal codes are two capital letters with no period (MA), the postal letters are, therefore, code letters, *not* abbreviations.

Numbers

Three procedures seem to be recommended for numbers. The writer may choose one of these. When you have chosen the method you prefer, use one and be consistent.

1. Write out the numbers when they can be expressed in one or two words, and write all others in Arabic: eleven, thirty-five, one hundred, 101, one thousand, and 20,410.

2. Write out numbers from one to ten, and put all other numbers in Arabic—that is, one through ten, 11, 12, 13, 14, etc.

3. Write out all numbers from one to ninety-nine, and use Arabic for all exact numbers 100 and above.

Two possible exceptions to the three rules are:

1. A number that begins a sentence is normally written out.

    Two hundred and five attended the book-buyers convention.

2. Always be consistent if numbers are being compared. For example:

    We didn't know whether to expect **seventy-five** or **one hundred and five** in that computer course.

15

The comma after the introductory element

This section attests to the great potential of the English language—a language that, because of the number of words and the complexity of its structure, has the capacity to convey the greatest variety of ideas in the history of civilization. Therefore, this chapter provides insight into ways to word and structure thoughts that might otherwise evade expression.

Whereas Rule 6 in Chapter 2 gives a general understanding of the introductory element, a study of this section of the book gives the user a more complex and versatile interpretation for conveying a variety of thoughts. For example, the writer may experience that an idea can be better expressed by organizing a phrase *or* a clause as the subject or the object of the main clause rather than by subordinating it to the main clause. Yes, it is technical and expressed in traditional terms. However, it is not beyond comprehension for those who want to become proficient in tonal variations and to produce the utmost in written expression.

An introductory element in a sentence may be a word, a phrase, or a dependent clause. *The introductory element offers variety in sentence structure.* It may offer a transitional expression; it may provide a mild interjection; it may, by transposing an ending phrase to an introductory position, even prevent ambiguity, as the second, "better" form of the following request illustrates.

Ambiguous:

> Would you please write the names of the students currently in your classes who will continue through the second semester **on the blank sign-up sheets I am distributing.**

Better*:*

> **On the blank sign-up sheets I am distributing,** would you please write the names of the students currently in your classes who will continue through the second semester.

Introductory phrases

Of the various sentence openings, the introductory phrase is the most common, primarily because of the several kinds of phrases that may introduce a sentence. Most of these phrases are followed by a comma; however, in some cases no comma is needed.

Simple prepositional phrase

Many of the introductory phrases are prepositional, and they may be either simple or complex in structure. The simple phrase contains a simple preposition, an object, and any adjective modifiers. You need not set off the simple introductory prepositional phrase with a comma unless the phrase is to be emphasized or unless the phrase might be misread without the comma.

In a few cases you will find a winner.

⇒ *Most simple introductory prepositional phrases do not need commas.*

Without any obligation, order your sample record today.

⇒ *This commonly used commercial phrase is intended to be emphasized.*

On the busy street, cars were jammed bumper to bumper.

⇒ *In this example the simple introductory prepositional phrase might have tripped up the reader were it not for the comma.*

Complex prepositional phrase

The introductory complex prepositional phrase may contain such combinations as two or more simple prepositional phrases, a preposition with either a gerund or infinitive phrase object, or a simple prepositional phrase with an adjective clause modifying the object of the preposition. Any one of these longer combinations is normally followed by a comma before the beginning of the main clause:

At the edge of the deep Maine woods near Moosehead Lake, he built a small log cabin.

⇒ *A complex introductory prepositional phrase, containing more than one prepositional phrase.*

By working in the dining hall, he was able to get through his second year of college.

⇒ *An introductory prepositional phrase, containing a gerund phrase—the gerund of which, in turn, has a prepositional phrase modifying it.*

In order to get service from the chattering waitresses, he tapped on his drinking glass.

⇒ *An introductory prepositional phrase, containing an infinitive phrase object—the infinitive of which has a prepositional phrase modifying it.*

In the room where he was hiding, we found the half-million dollars that was stolen in the bank holdup.

⇒ *An introductory prepositional phrase containing a dependent clause.*

Verbal phrase

Of the three kinds of verbals—gerund, participle, or infinitive—two form phrases that as sentence openers must be followed by a comma. The first of these is the participial phrase, which is used as an adjective; the other is the adjective infinitive phrase:

Having been interrupted by all the merriment, he decided to give up the idea of studying and join the crowd.

⇒ *An introductory participial phrase.*

To be sure that he would always be on time, Ted made it a rule to set his alarm clock a half-hour ahead every night.

⇒ *An introductory infinitive phrase.*

Be sure that you do not put a comma after a gerund phrase that is the subject of a verb because a single comma is rarely placed between a subject and verb. (The instance in which two like verbs appear together is an exception to this rule, however: *Whatever will be, will be.*) The same present participle that forms a participial phrase also makes a gerund phrase.

> **Walking through the woods** can be fun and educational, too.
>
> ⇒ *Gerund phrase is the subject of the verb* can be—*no comma!*

> **Walking through the woods,** we noticed that the oak trees could withstand storm and ice far better than any of the other trees.
>
> ⇒ *Participial phrase modifies the subject* we.

Also, a comma is unnecessary after an infinitive phrase that is the subject of a verb.

> **To provide for his large family** was his only concern.
>
> ⇒ *Infinitive phrase is the subject of the verb* was—*no comma!*

Absolute phrase

A variation of the phrases constructed with verbals are the phrases traditionally known as absolutes. An absolute phrase usually consists of a noun or pronoun with either a participial modifier or an adjective infinitive modifier. Occasionally, the absolute phrase may be an adverb infinitive. The absolute phrase may also be an expression clarifying the attitude or the intention of the writer. Because the introductory absolute phrase is independent of the clause before which it appears, you must always set it off with a comma.

> **The ballots being counted by an impartial committee,** we were certain that the results would be fair.

⇒ *An absolute, containing a noun modified by a participial phrase.*

> **The work yet to be completed,** we went home.

⇒ *An absolute, containing a noun modified by an infinitive phrase.*

> **To be exact**, the blueprint must be drawn up by a professional.

⇒ *This absolute is an infinitive phrase used parenthetically.*

> **Generally speaking,** superior intelligence does not necessarily make one a good teacher.

⇒ *This absolute is an ungrammatical expression clarifying the attitude of the writer.*

An introductory absolute *without* a verbal is also set off by a comma.

> **The cat out for the night,** we started to go to bed.

Adjective cluster phrase

Often a writer uses an introductory adjective with its modifiers to modify a noun or pronoun in the independent clause. This combination we will call an adjective phrase with modifiers, the modifiers of which may be phrasal or clausal. There seems to be no traditional name for it, but today's grammarians are beginning to call it an "adjective phrase with an adjective headword" or an "adjective cluster." You must also separate this construction from the main clause with a comma.

> **Aware of all her failings,** he asked Nellie to marry him.

⇒ *The adjective* aware *with its prepositional phrase modifier* of all her failings *makes an adjective cluster that modifies the subject of the independent clause,* he.

> **Certain that he would have plenty of time,** Marty took six subjects instead of the customary four.

⇒ *Here the adjective* certain *with its adjective clause modifiers makes an adjective cluster that modifies* Marty, *the subject of the independent clause.*

Introductory clauses

Another kind of introductory element, the adverb clause, is very effective in providing sentence structure with emphasis and variety. In this transposed position (before the independent clause in a complex sentence), the adverbial clause is normally followed by a comma. A subordinate conjunction (see pages 183-184) is always the first word in the adverbial clause.

> **Although his first book on punctuation was written more than a hundred years ago,** John Wilson emphasized rules that are as applicable to 20th-century writing as they were to 19th-century prose.

If the sentence is rather short, then the writer may prefer to omit the comma after the introductory element.

> **If you are available** please fill in and return the application.

No matter how short the sentence is, if clarity is at stake, a comma is used after the introductory adverb clause to avoid misreading. For example, only a careless writer would omit the comma in the following sentences:

> **As we ate,** the pups played under the table.

> **While I was shaving,** my wife prepared me a quick lunch.

Although most introductory clauses are adverbial—that is, dependent clauses introduced by subordinate conjunctions—there is an occasional absolute clause. As implied previously, absolutes have no grammatical relationship to the main clause and are related only in meaning to the rest of the sentence.

> **Whatever happens,** we must not fail him.

> **Whoever it is,** let him wait his turn.

Note that—as in the case of the noun or gerund phrases on page 167—you do not put a comma after a noun clause that is the subject of a verb, because a single comma is rarely placed between a subject and a verb.

Why the colors are sometimes distorted cannot be adequately explained by the television experts.

⇒ *There is no comma between the noun-clause subject and the verb.*

When two like verbs appear together—one ending the noun clause and the other the verb of the main clause—there is an exception:

Whoever it is, is too late.

But this does not mean that two unlike verbs appearing together will be separated by a comma.

Whoever it is will be too late.

Furthermore, there are instances in which two like words will appear together not separated by commas, such as when the verb *have* appears in the past perfect tense.

If I **had had** the book, I could have studied the lesson.

An introductory phrase or clause may appear before any independent clause whether that independent clause is a simple sentence, part of a complex sentence, or part of a compound sentence.

Introductory elements to simple and complex sentences have been thoroughly discussed. Now let us observe examples of an introductory clause and an introductory phrase set before the second of two independent clauses in compound and compound-complex sentences.

We will be there on time; **but if you are late,** we will not be able to wait.

The second of the two independent clauses is introduced by an adverbial clause. Note that there is no comma before *if* in order to permit smooth reading after the break at the coordinate conjunction.

After struggling through a year and a half of trying to make the business school pay, he decided to resign; **and transferring all his responsibilities to his partner,** he accepted the new teaching position.

⇒ *Observe the participial phrase before the second of the two independent clauses. Also note the introductory adverbial phrase before the first independent clause.*

Punctuation of introductory words—such as *obviously, yes, oh, in the meantime*—can be studied in the chapter on the comma. Additional illustrations of introductory terms with appositive forms can be found in chapters on the comma, the dash, the colon, and the semicolon.

Other kinds of introductory elements are merely variations of syntactical combinations already discussed, as the first two examples on page 90 illustrate. These two examples were made possible by innovative uses of the dash developed in the last 50 years. There is always the possibility that writers—in their constant search for variety, flexibility, and versatility in expressing ideas—may continue to create new kinds of structural sentence patterns, especially with all the innovations that have been made possible with the computer.

Glossary

Authors' note: Normally, one book alone would not cover all the grammatical terms in the English language. Therefore, in keeping with the objective of providing a book of "punctuation, plain and simple," the glossary in this book has been narrowed down to those grammatical terms that are most relevant to a layman's study of punctuation.

absolute expression. An absolute expression is a clausal or phrasal expression that functions independently and is related to the context in thought while remaining grammatically unrelated to the independent clause.

> **The ballots being counted by an impartial committee,** we were certain that the results would be fair.
> **The work yet to be completed,** we went home.

adverbial clause. An adverbial clause is one that is connected to the independent clause by a subordinate conjunction and modifies the verb in the independent clause or the whole independent clause.

> **Although his first book on punctuation was written more than 100 years ago,** John Wilson emphasized rules that are as applicable to 20th-century writing as they were to 19th-century prose.

adjective cluster. An adjective cluster consists of one main adjective and its modifiers. It is also known as an adjective phrase.

Danny was **conscious of her presence**.
Conscious of her presence, Danny acted very awkwardly.

ampersand. An abbreviated form of the word *and*. The sign & (sometimes called an abbreviation) is frequently used in company names.

appositive. An appositive is used to further explain a noun or a group of words to which it is adjunct, and it normally appears after the word or words it renames. It usually consists of a noun with modifiers and, when nonessential, is set off with commas.

Mr. Thompson, **our butcher,** is on vacation.

clause. A clause is a group of closely related words with a subject and a verb and may be either independent or dependent. The types of dependent clauses are noun, adjective, adverb, and absolute.

close punctuation. (See "open and close punctuation.")

comma splice. A comma splice or "comma fault" is an error in punctuation committed in instances where a writer often erroneously separates two independent elements with a comma rather than with the proper mark of punctuation, which can be a semicolon, a period, or a comma followed by a coordinate conjunction.

composite adjective. A composite adjective— sometimes called a noncoordinate adjective— is one of a series of adjectives, each of which in turn modifies the remaining composites *with the noun.* Composite adjectives do not separately modify the noun as do coordinate adjectives. (In the phrase *a dingy white shirt*, while *dingy* does modify *shirt*, it more specifically modifies *white shirt*.)

conjunction. Conjunctions (or "connectors," as they are sometimes called) join words, phrases, or clauses. (See "coordinate conjunction" and "subordinate conjunction.")

conjunctive adverb. A conjunctive adverb joins two independent clauses and functions as an adverb within the second clause. The following is a list of the most commonly used conjunctive adverbs:

accordingly	for instance	moreover
adversely	furthermore	namely
after all	hence	nevertheless
also	however	next
anyhow	in addition	nonetheless
anyway	in any event	notwithstanding
as a result	in contrast	now
at any rate	in fact	on the contrary
at least	in other words	on the other
besides	in short	hand
by and large	in the meantime	otherwise
by far	inasmuch	similarly
consequently	indeed	still
even so	instead	then
finally	likewise	therefore
for example	meanwhile	thus

The conjunctive adverbs that connect two main clauses are usually punctuated with a semicolon preceding the word or term. Except the one-syllable conjunctive adverbs and the word *also*, each is then followed by a comma.

These words may also be used as simple adverbs and appear parenthetically within a clause. They may also be the first word of a sentence, contributing to a more coherent paragraph.

coordinate adjective. A coordinate adjective relates directly to the noun or pronoun it modifies. In a series of coordinate adjectives, each of the adjectives is equal to and parallel with any other adjective in that series and modifies only the noun or pronoun that the series of coordinate adjectives seeks to qualify (*tall, handsome, virile lifeguard*).

coordinate conjunction. A coordinate conjunction links parallel or equal words, phrases, or clauses. There are nine commonly used coordinate conjunctions: *and, but, or, nor, for, so, yet, while,* and *whereas.*

correlative conjunction. Correlative conjunctions are actually coordinate conjunctions used in pairs to indicate comparison or contrast between two equal or parallel words, phrases, or clauses. The most common of these are *either/or, neither/nor, whether/or, not only/but, not only/but also,* and *both/and.*

declarative sentence. A declarative sentence is one that makes an assertion. Its terminal mark is a period.

dependent clause. (See "dependent element.")

dependent element. A dependent element is a phrase or a clause that does not in itself contain a comprehensive thought. It, therefore, cannot stand alone but must be linked to an independent element.

ellipsis. An ellipsis (plural *ellipses)* is the omission of a word or words from a sentence. In dialogue the omitted words may be obvious, but in expository writing the omission is usually indicated by dots— three dots at the beginning of or within a sentence and four dots if the omission extends to the end of the sentence.

exclamatory sentence. An exclamatory sentence is one that denotes surprise, horror, or any other strong emotion. Such sentences are punctuated with exclamation marks.

expletives. The meaningless words *there* and *it* allow the writer to manipulate words in other than a subject/predicate pattern. Expletives may help avoid awkward sentence structures. These two words appear at the beginning of a sentence to delay the subject.

> It is snowing outside. (Snowing is going on outside.)
> There are too many bugs in June. (Too many bugs are in June.)

There are five jets flying in formation overhead. (Five jets are flying overhead in formation. *Or:* Overhead are five jets, flying in formation.)

homograph. Two or more words spelled alike but having different functions in the context of one's writing. Good examples of homographs are the pronouns *his*, which can be an adjective, possessive pronoun, or a pronoun, standing alone; the pronoun *her*, which can be an objective case noun or a possessive pronoun; and the pronoun *it*, which can be subjective or objective (see "personal pronouns" in this glossary). Another good example is the verb *is*, which can be a helping verb, a linking verb, or an intransitive verb. Really, there is not one *is* but three *is*'s, homographically speaking.

imperative sentence. An imperative sentence is one that gives a command or a request or indicates that something is to be done. In such sentences the subject *you* or *will you* is often omitted and is said "to be understood." An imperative sentence ends with a period.

indefinite pronoun. Unlike all other pronouns, indefinite pronouns usually do not have antecedents, and they function more like nouns than pronouns. Indefinite pronouns that are considered singular include:

anybody	no one
anyone	nobody
anything	nothing
each one	somebody
everybody	someone
everyone	something
everything	

When used alone as subjects, the following words would also be considered singular indefinite pronouns:

another	little
each	much
either	neither

If used alone in a sentence— that is, like nouns and not like adjectives— the following would be considered plural indefinite pronouns:

> any
> both
> few
> many

The following are either singular or plural, depending on the context in which they appear:

> all of
> most of
> none of
> some of

> Most of the pie has been eaten.
> None of the people were here.

(Please note that the *indefinite* pronoun is the only pronoun that forms its possessive like a noun by adding an apostrophe before the *s* (*'s*) for the singular form.

independent element. An independent element is a clause containing both a subject and a predicate. It expresses a complete thought and thus can be a sentence in itself.

infinitive phrase. An infinitive can function as a noun, an adjective, or an adverb. It is made up of the word *to* plus a form of a verb. The infinitive is usually part of a phrase that is used as a noun, an adjective, or an adverb. For example, when an infinitive is part of an adverb phrase, the whole phrase with the infinitive modifies the independent clause.

> **To achieve the highest standards possible,** the school board hired the best teachers available.

The infinitive phrase *to achieve* modifies the independent clause.

interjection. An interjection is a brief exclamation— often consisting of only one or two words— used to indicate an impromptu emotional response. If it is part of a sentence, it is usually followed by a comma; more generally, however, it is followed by an exclamation mark.

> **Horrors!** What a long, drawn-out lecture!
> **Oh,** don't act so hastily.

interrogative. An interrogative sentence is one which asks a question and is punctuated with a question mark.

intonation. Intonation is a general term encompassing changes in pitch, degrees of stress, internal and terminal juncture, and overall rhythms of speech.

nonrestrictive element. A nonrestrictive element is one that adds detail to the sentence in which it appears, but it can be omitted from that sentence without changing the basic meaning.

open and close punctuation. The style of punctuation that uses as few marks as possible is called "open punctuation"; while the style of punctuation that puts to use every mark that can be justified, whether or not it is needed, is called "close punctuation."

parenthetical element or expression. A parenthetical expression (sometimes called an "interrupter") may be a word, a phrase, or a clause and may be omitted from a sentence without affecting the basic meaning. It may be set off from the sentence by commas, by dashes, or by parentheses.

personal pronouns. The following are examples of personal pronouns:

> **Singular:**
> I; me; my (possessive of a noun); mine (possessive alone)
> you; your (poss. with a noun); yours (poss. alone)
> she; her (objectively used); her (poss. with noun);
>   hers (poss. alone)
> he; him; his (poss. of a noun); his (poss. alone)
> it (subjective); it (objective); its (poss. of noun)

Plural:
we; us; our (poss. of noun); ours (poss. alone)
you; your; yours (same as sing.)
they; their (poss. of noun); theirs (poss. alone)

The possessives *yours, hers, its, ours,* and *theirs* never need apostrophes. *Its* only takes an apostrophe when it is a contraction of *it is.*

Is the book his or **hers**?

Those wooden Tinker Toys are **ours.**

The cat hurt **its** paw.

It's your party.

Don't you know **it's** bedtime? *(Or if you're referring to the cat:* Don't you know **its** bedtime?*)*

Personal pronouns and indefinite pronouns are alike in that both take the place of a noun. The indefinite pronoun is more like a noun in that it forms its possessive with *'s* and is normally singular; the personal pronoun forms its possessive by changing its form. For example:

>*one* to *one's, everybody* to *everybody's,* etc.

but

>*he* and *him* to *his, she* and *her* to *her* and *hers, it* to *its, they* and *them* to *their* and *theirs,* etc.

prepositional phrase. A preposition is a word that shows relationship between the noun or pronoun that follows it (the object) and some other word in the sentence. The preposition, its objects, and the modifiers of that object make up a prepositional phrase that either modifies the noun or the pronoun to which the preposition relates its object or completes and qualifies the idea carried forward through a verb.

The house **on the hill** is red.

The red house is **on the hill.**

Sometimes a preposition may introduce a prepositional phrase used as a noun.

> He climbed **to within 30 feet of the peak of Mt. Tom.**

> **From across the lake** she could hear the band playing her favorite dance music.

The prepositional phrase as a unit may also be a predicate adjective.

> This particular study of the American language is **of utmost importance.**

When two or more prepositional phrases are combined, they become a complex prepositional phrase. Therefore, this lengthy group of words— when introducing an independent clause— must be followed by a comma.

> **By working in the dining room,** he was able to get through his second year of college.

> **In order to get service from the chattering waitresses,** he tapped on his drinking glass.

There are simple prepositions, compound prepositions, and phrasal prepositions. The following is a list of the three types of prepositions:

Simple prepositions:

aboard	around	by
about	as	concerning
above	at	considering
across	before	despite
after	behind	during
against	below	except
along	beneath	following
alongside	beside	for
amid	between	from
amidst	beyond	in
among	but (except)	inside

into	over	toward
like	past	under
near	per	until
notwithstanding	round	upon
of	since	via
off	through	with
on	throughout	within
onto	till	without
opposite	to	

Compound prepositions:

according to	due to
ahead of	in back of
apart from	out of
apropos of	over against
as to	owing to
back of	together with
because of	up to
contrary to	

Phrasal prepositions:

as far as	in spite of
by reason of	in the event of
in accordance with	in view of
in addition to	on account of
in place of	with reference to
in regard to	with regard to
in respect to	

poetry. In contrast to prose, poetry— because of its differing aspects of subject matter, form, and effect— defies definition. Poetry can express feelings and thoughts beyond the greatest potential of prose.

prose. Prose is all writing that is not poetry. Generally, prose is any expository writing that explains. Prose includes all nonfiction such as essays, articles, journals, editorials, newspaper reporting, biographies— the list is limitless. Prose also includes all fiction.

prosody. Prosody refers to a rhythmic pattern that permits words to flow freely or rhythmically.

restrictive element. A restrictive element is one that is essential to the basic meaning of a sentence; and for the most accurate interpretation, the restrictive element cannot be omitted.

> I suspected **that the revising of** this manuscript would take weeks to finish.

> The editor **who knows the rules of grammar and punctuation** has been given the project.

sentence. A sentence expresses one complete thought. If it is less than or more than a complete thought, it is not a sentence. The fact that a sentence has a subject and a predicate is only incidental; what is most important is that it have a so-called "oneness" of thought.

sentence fragment. Traditionally, a sentence fragment is a group of words that intends to convey a complete thought but does not satisfy the requirements of a structurally complete sentence. Most fragmentary sentences cannot adequately justify their uses, but some forms (such as exclamatory remarks and ellipses) can be more effective than complete sentences. Many advertisements break the rules and tend to get attention by doing so. In the latter, fragments are related to fragments to get a complete thought in context.

sic. A Latin word meaning "thus it is." It is often enclosed in brackets and inserted into a quotation to distinguish a mistake or unbelieved fact stated by the individual quoted.

subordinate conjunction. Subordinate conjunctions are connectors that not only introduce adverb clauses and some noun clauses, but also tie these elements to independent clauses. Following is a list of the most commonly used subordinate conjunctions:

according	as far as	as though
after	as if	because
although	as long as	before
as	as soon as	even if

except	provided	until
how	provided that	when
however (no	so	whence
matter how)	so that	whenever
in order that	than	where
lest	through	whereas
no matter	till	while
once	unless	why

syntax. Syntax is the orderly arrangement of word groups and their interrelationships within a sentence.

tag. An interruption within quoted material, such as dialogue, to give a name to the speaker is called a "tag."

> "Be on time!" **he scolded.** "Or next time you will be marked absent."

transitional element. A transitional element is a word or a group of words used to bridge the gap between two separate ideas, two independent elements, or a combination of elements. A transitional element— such as a conjunctive adverb— tends to give coherence to prose (see list on page 175).

verbal. A verbal looks like a verb and acts like a verb, but it is not a verb *per se* because a verb with a subject makes a complete sentence. A verbal needs a helping verb in a sentence, or it has to be part of a phrase. These phrases often require commas to punctuate them. For a complete study of the punctuation of the verbals— the gerund, participial, and infinitive phrases— along with prepositional, absolute, and cluster phrases (see Chapter 15).

Index